Praise for *Dog Lessons* by Hersch Wilson

"Part meditation and part memoir, *Dog Lessons* takes readers off-leash to discover how our canine companions can unleash wildness, serenity, and joy."

— **Gary Kowalski**, author of *Goodbye, Friend: Healing Wisdom for Anyone Who Has Ever Lost a Pet*

"In *Dog Lessons*, Hersch Wilson ponders the canine-human bond and looks back on a long life enhanced at each step of the way by the dogs at his side. Each chapter feels like an engaging walk in the woods, with easy conversation that flows from nostalgic tales to bits of history to meditations on interconnectedness — all of it centered on what dogs can teach us, if only we slow down enough to pay attention."

— **Kathy Callahan**, author of *101 Rescue Puppies* and *Welcoming Your Puppy from Planet Dog*

"In *Dog Lessons*, dog lover and master storyteller Hersch Wilson shows how our canine companions can teach us many valuable life lessons if we allow them to do so and to express their dogness. *Dog Lessons* also will make readers think about who dogs are, what they need to have dog-rich lives, and how to make dog-human relationships the best they can be."

— **Marc Bekoff**, author of *Dogs Demystified: An A-to-Z Guide to All Things Canine*, *Unleashing Your Dog* (with Jessica Pierce), and *The Emotional Lives of Animals*

"*Dog Lessons* is a truly beautiful book and a must-have for any dog lover's library. It's the kind of book that makes you want to snuggle your furry best friend closer than ever out of gratitude and awe. After all, as author Hersch Wilson observes, our dogs teach us so many brilliant lessons in life: napping is wonderful, dog walks *always* make everything better, and 'Woods, River, Dog' is an excellent recipe for a happy life."

— **Laura T. Coffey,** author of the national bestseller *My Old Dog: Rescued Pets with Remarkable Second Acts*

Dog
Lessons

Also by Hersch Wilson

Firefighter Zen: A Field Guide to Thriving in Tough Times

Play to Win: Choosing Growth over Fear in Work and Life
(coauthored with Larry Wilson)

Test of Faith: A Novel of Faith and Murder in the Southwest

Dog Lessons

Learning the Important Stuff
from Our Best Friends

HERSCH WILSON

Illustrations by Dan Bodelson

New World Library
Novato, California

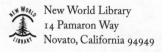

New World Library
14 Pamaron Way
Novato, California 94949

Text design by Tona Pearce Myers

Library of Congress Cataloging-in-Publication Data

Names: Wilson, Hersch, author.
Title: Dog lessons : learning the important stuff from our best friends / Hersch Wilson ; illustrations by Dan Bodelson.
Description: Novato, California : New World Library, [2023] | Includes bibliographical references. | Summary: "A collection of stories about the human-dog relationship. Drawing on his personal experience, the author explores the lessons that dogs can teach us about love, loyalty, courage, grief, and joyfully living in the present. Each chapter discusses a different lesson and its relevance to our own lives"-- Provided by publisher.
Identifiers: LCCN 2023021252 (print) | LCCN 2023021253 (ebook) | ISBN 9781608688876 (hardback) | ISBN 9781608688883 (epub)
Subjects: LCSH: Dogs--Anecdotes. | Human-animal relationships--Anecdotes. | Dog owners--Psychology--Anecdotes.
Classification: LCC SF426.2 .W545 2023 (print) | LCC SF426.2 (ebook) |DDC 636.7--dc23/eng/20230615
LC record available at https://lccn.loc.gov/2023021252
LC ebook record available at https://lccn.loc.gov/2023021253

First printing, September 2023
ISBN 978-1-60868-887-6
Ebook ISBN 978-1-60868-888-3
Printed in Canada on 100% postconsumer-waste recycled paper

New World Library is proud to be a Gold Certified Environmentally Responsible Publisher. Publisher certification awarded by Green Press Initiative.

10 9 8 7 6 5 4 3 2 1

As an introspective ten-year-old, I was perfectly content staying in my room. (I had four sisters, all younger, so you may understand my motivation.) My mom came in one morning, saw me, and had an insight. She said, "Hey, we should get a dog." And that changed everything. This book is dedicated to my mom, Ann Nugent Wilson.

CONTENTS

Writer's Note xiii

Dog Spirit 1
DOG LESSON: On Love 8

Part 1: First Dog

… And She Threw Up on My Shoes 15
DOG LESSON: Getting Over Poop 19
Save the Puppies! 21
"Free Love" 26
The Legacy of Little Joe 29
DOG LESSON: Freedom 35
Wildness 37
DOG LESSON: Wild at Heart 45
When a Wild Place Disappears 48

Part 2: Philosophy of Dog

The Great Horned Owl 58
DOG LESSON: How to Not Get into a Fight 63
We Live in a World of Sentience 66
DOG LESSON: The Importance of Touch 71
A Dog's Reality 72
It's Not Just about the Breed 78
DOG LESSON: The Importance of Naps 87
Loving-Kindness 88
What Happened to the Wallpaper? 95

Part 3: Living in Wild Country

The Road to Santa Fe   105

In the Wilderness   113

DOG LESSON: Keep It Simple   118

Is It a Good Idea to Have Three Dogs and a Baby
in the Wilderness?   120

DOG LESSON: Masters of What Is Important   128

Zuni Just Wants to Run   130

DOG LESSON: Coyote Fit   136

Childhood Is the Kingdom Where No One Ever Dies   138

DOG LESSON: Zoomies   143

Part 4: Life with Berners!

Enjoy Chaos? Adopt Bernese Mountain Dog Puppies   151

Let the Dogs Out, Let the Dogs In …   160

DOG LESSON: Escaping   165

"Good Nellie, Good Girl"   167

DOG LESSON: Calm Human, Calm Dog   172

Off-Leash in the Mountains   174

When an Old Dog Dies   180

DOG LESSON: How to Be Old   186

Part 5: Wait … We Have a Chihuahua?

No Little Dog Is Going to Win My Heart …   192

Rescuing Maisie   197

DOG LESSON: Get Down on Your Belly
and Investigate the Tall Grass   203

We Lied about Never Getting Another Big Dog   205

When a Dire Wolf Runs Across a Golf Course   211

DOG LESSON: Resilience   220
Maisie and Toby Versus the Coyotes   223
DOG LESSON: Bravery   228

Part 6: Final Lessons

The Trial of the Pig   235
Dogs of Ukraine   243
Walking in the Universe   247
DOG LESSON: When There Is Nothing to Do,
    It's Okay to Do Nothing   253
The World Is a Very Narrow Bridge   254

Acknowledgments   261
Sources   263
About the Author   271

WRITER'S NOTE

Four things.

First, I am originally from Minnesota. This is an important writer insight. The second-largest religion in Minnesota, south of Lutheranism, is self-deprecation. In 1997, when the University of Minnesota men's basketball team made it to the NCAA Final Four and then were defeated by Kentucky, a friend commented, "It's better that way. We're not winners, we are a solid number three."

By the way, when searching for the facts under "U of M," Google took me to the University of Miami, which I find fitting. Minnesotans don't often wave our own flag.

The dark secret underneath self-deprecation is the belief that if the world would just do things *our way*, it would be a better place. Because we are a polite people, that judgy, opinionated stuff usually comes out sideways, which is also our way.

This is a winding road to say, in writing about our amazing companions, dogs, if I come off as saying, "Do it this way!" I apologize, deeply, in advance.

Next, the opinions expressed are mine. As Yogi Berra said, "I can't write about your opinion. It's not mine!" (Okay, he never said that, but it sounds about right.)

Third, about the science presented in the book. When I was a freshman at Colorado College, I took introduction to physical anthropology. It was a wonderful and special gift to take that class.

But the professors leaned hard into their certainty that anthropology was settled science. Then, in 1974, "Lucy" (*Australopithecus afarensis*) was discovered, and in 2010 an even older *A. afarensis* was found. These discoveries upended the established "facts" I was taught about human evolution, forced new theories, and created all sorts of new lesson plans for undergraduates.

The point is, I present the science in this book as "provisional approximations," to quote Antonio Damasio (*Descartes' Error*). This is nowhere truer than in emerging sciences like animal cognition. Much that we currently "know" about dogs is likely to change.

Fourth, and finally, I've come to realize that if you don't have your world turned upside down and learn new things by writing a book, then you've missed the point of writing. Writing changes the writer.

My best analogy comes from walking down our road after a wet summer. We now live in New Mexico, and when the desert blooms, it is astonishing. What first captured my eyes are the garish blooms, the Adonis blazing stars, the prairie verbena, and the fields of sunflowers. Then I once looked a little closer and discovered these small, separate, blood-bright red flowers — which after a little "research" turned out to be wild morning glories — using the garish flowers as scaffolding. I followed their tangled vines to the soil and discovered grasses that I'd never seen before and mosses that were not there yesterday. Bees, beetles, and ants swarmed everywhere. I dug my hands into the soil and noted that it was organic and full of unseeable life.

In doing so — maybe it's just me — I realized I know nothing about the wild world that envelops me.

Diving into the world of dogs, being with them, asking of them questions, reading the works of brilliant canine thinkers — Alexandra Horowitz, Temple Grandin, Virginia Morell, and of course, the writer and veterinarian James Herriot — it is the same experience. One observation begets another and another. My held concept of dogs, of animals, is shattered and rebuilt and the journey continues.

So. If readers didn't exist, I would have never found myself with what I now consider special knowledge. Thus to you, thank you, thank you.

To break the ice between us, here are a few need-to-knows about me, my family, and our dogs:

1. Yes, our dogs sleep on our furniture.
2. Yes, we live with lots of dog hair and are unnaturally obsessed with vacuum cleaners.
3. Yes, we kiss our dogs.
4. Our dogs are insistent about living an indoor/outdoor life.
5. You will note that this book has a distinct "country" flavor. I've lived in cities in the United States, Canada, and Europe, but I am at heart someone who needs *space*. It's my mom's fault.
6. Our main topics of conversation are kids, dogs, and food. In my family, it is accepted to interrupt any conversation, even life-and-death conversations, with a request to pass the ketchup.

7. My high-level life advice — because at age seventy-three, I'm often asked for advice — for almost any calamity is, when in doubt, *walk your dog*. When you return, you will have a better idea of whether you have a problem or just an inconvenience. Don't just sit there!

Let's begin.

Dog Spirit

This is what you shall do:
Love the earth and sun and the animals.

— Walt Whitman, *Leaves of Grass*

"What do you want for dinner?" I shouted above the din.

My daughter Sully and I were standing next to each other in our hallway. We had our faces and bodies smashed up against the wall.

We were having difficulty hearing each other, and we were holding our arms and possessions over our heads, much like when you're arrested.

But it wasn't the police. The cause was two eight-month-old, wild Bernese mountain dog puppies who were just unbelievably excited to see us. They were raucously loud, sprinting up and down the hallway bringing us toys, coffee cups, the TV remote, all as their way of saying, *Welcome home! We bring you presents! We missed you so much!*

Perfectly normal for us.

To the initiated, *the obsessed dog people*, you must be thinking, well, this family did not do the requisite training.

You'd be right.

We tried and tried and failed. More about that later.

I

Yet coming home and being overwhelmed with love has its benefits. It's hard to be in a bad mood when a dog (or two) is expressing undying affection for you.

For the nine years Nellie and Tank lived with us, before they passed, each day began with a walk, one that was normally exciting and sometimes anxiety provoking because I never knew what would happen. Once, in front of a new house construction site, Tank spied a dead rabbit on the road. Enlisting Nellie — both were then about 130 pounds — they towed me to the rabbit as I struggled to hold them back. Tank pounced on it, and I pounced on Tank and grabbed the rabbit, and we wrestled for possession — I was afraid the rabbit might have died from the disease tularemia! All work on the new house ceased as the construction guys watched in amazement as a sixty-two-year-old guy rolled on the ground with two bear-like dogs over a dead rabbit. After a struggle I won, I held the rabbit over my head. Misinterpreting the gesture — I was just trying to keep the rabbit away from the dogs — the construction guys applauded and hooted.

We unapologetically spoil our dogs. They give so much, and we want them to be as happy, content, and *dog-like* as possible. We want them to be dogs, not possessions or little humans; dogs, not trained robots; dogs, members of our family. Our dogs often follow us from room to room; we seem always together.

We do draw the line at rolling in deer poop or, God forbid, eating dog poop. I have asked numerous veterinarians why dogs eat dog poop; no one has a good answer. Other than those, our rules are rather lax.

After our hallway greeting, the Bernese puppies followed us into the kitchen. There, as we began to cook, they lay down to be as close to us as possible. Berners are notorious for turning into "lumps" on the floor, not moving and content for humans just to step over or around them. So we let them be and got on with making dinner. We did it automatically; no sense trying to shoo them out, they'd just come right back. Of course, why would we? We have always considered our dogs as part of our family web, napping alongside us while we work or do chores. We are close knit. And evenings are best. A warm kitchen, happy dogs, and content humans.

A theme of this book is that the world is a complex and often frightening place. To keep our sense of purpose and our sanity, we must be engaged, we must fight the battles, being kind in a world that can seem uncaring. We also need refuge, quiet, peace, and especially love. Being in a house suffused with dog spirit gives us that. Dogs give more than they take. With a little caring, stirring in time with them, walks, runs, play, and belly rubs, they will return the love tenfold.

Love, Statistics, and Science

I am not a dog trainer, a noble and needed profession, and this is not a training manual. Nor am I a dog cognition expert, an exploding field focused on understanding our first nonhuman companions, and this is not a survey of dog science. Rather, I am a dog *guardian* in possibly the fortieth millennia of our relationship with dogs: a cool and hallowed responsibility. This book is about living with dogs and what we might learn from them.

I have lived with dogs for sixty years or so. In that time, my relationship with dogs has gone through multiple phases. I've gone from being wondrous at having a first dog, to appreciating their loyalty, to taking them for granted, to again being wondrous. In writing this book, doing the research, remembering times with dogs who have passed, and spending time with our current dogs — Toby, a Great Pyrenees mix, and Maisie, a Chihuahua-whatever mix — I have been nothing if not astonished by their resilience and affection. Consider this book also my unabashed love letter to dogs.

Of course, dogs are not perfect. As I write this, I'm in Minnesota at my daughter's home, and Toby is at home in New Mexico with a dog sitter. I assume, because we are not there, he has escaped four times in as many days, opening doors, breaking through screens, vaulting walls, diving out of windows, and showing up at our extremely patient neighbors.

Next: shoes. Stuck in traffic, I once tried to calculate the damage dogs do to the economy by destroying shoes — a common occurrence over the years with us. Roughly, there are seventy million US households with dogs. Let's say, on average, each household has one dog that destroys at least one pair of shoes each year. To make it easy, let's say a pair of shoes costs on average fifty dollars. Yes, I know, this underestimates the cost of many shoes, but it makes sitting in a car doing math easier. That comes out to $3.5 billion a year in damaged shoes.

More seriously, dog attacks account for between thirty

and forty deaths each year in the US. Most attacks are by dogs who are loose and running free, not socialized, often in packs, and who are not desexed.

To keep this in perspective, snakes kill around ten individuals each year (out of seven thousand or so venomous bites). Since 1890, there have been twenty-seven people killed by mountain lions (I'm obsessed by mountain lions), and approximately twenty people are killed by cows, *yes cows*, each year. Of course, the biggest predators worldwide are mosquitoes (750,000 deaths per year) and us! On average, we clock in at 437,000 humans killed each year (not including wars).

About dog attacks. My youngest daughter, Sully, vociferously declares that it's not dogs but stupid people who are mostly responsible for attacks. That is, she often clarifies impatiently, it is bad dog "owners" who should not be allowed near any animal.

She is much more radical than I.

Of course, Mark Twain famously wrote that "there are lies, damn lies, and statistics." Or as my wife, Laurie, constantly reminds me, if you're the one who is attacked, statistics are meaningless.

How much do dogs know? Well, for one thing, dogs fail the "mirror" test. This is an experiment designed to see if animals can recognize themselves in a mirror, thus demonstrating self-awareness. Dolphins, the great apes, a single Asiatic elephant, and magpies pass the mirror test. However, this sight-centric test does not involve or account for a dog's primary sense, smell. If there was a mirror test using scent, I bet they'd be brilliant.

Dog Lessons

I feel the subtitle of this book — "Learning the Important Stuff from Our Best Friends" — needs some explanation. First, to be contrarian, there are a lot of important things that dogs can't teach us. For example, in high school, having a dog that could have taught me calculus or Spanish would have been a significant help in my quest to get into college and thus avoid the draft. Also, contrary to stories about Lassie and other dogs who find their way home over hundreds of miles, not all dogs are great navigators. Only approximately 30 percent of lost dogs find their way home. I sympathize with this. As a firefighter, I was once voted "most likely to get lost on the way to a call."

Yet I have found that math, Spanish, and navigation, while helpful, are not essential life skills.

What can dogs teach us? A lot, particularly about being social animals. Humans and dogs have both evolved to survive in small groups, whether those communities are called packs, tribes, clans, families, or kinship groups.

Vital dog lessons for us include love, loyalty, curiosity, how to avoid serious fights, wildness, and zoomies, among others. Not a bad list for a good life. We could all do better with less conflict, a couple of naps, and more playtime. I've highlighted these skills in "Dog Lesson" sections throughout.

A final note. There is one fact that all dog people hold in their hearts. A dog's life is much shorter than ours. In our garden we have a tree with a little stone marker on which is written "Zuni's Tree." Zuni was a German shepherd that lived with us for eight years. He was hit and killed by a car.

We grieved for months after he passed. Now we have Toby, a Great Pyrenees, who howls every time he hears coyotes, fire department sirens, or the theme music for *Modern Family*. (We watched a lot of TV reruns during the Covid-19 lockdowns.) A meta-lesson that dogs teach is that life with dogs is joyous and short. From dogs we learn that even the happiest of lives are threaded with sadness. That is the largest of lessons that dogs teach.

On Love

A love story. Argos was the dog of Odysseus. As Homer wrote in the Odyssey, Odysseus leaves the kingdom of Ithaca, and Argos, to fight the Trojan wars, and it takes him twenty years to return. Upon arrival home, he disguises himself, since the palace is filled with hostile suitors for his wife, Penelope.

Yet Argos, old and infested by fleas, recognizes Odysseus, wags his tail, and stands up on shaky legs. Odysseus cannot give away who he is, so he passes by Argos without a word, yet legend has it he sheds a tear.

In that moment, Argos lies down and dies.

Later, I discuss the biochemistry of love and the evolution of the dog-human relationship, including of course our love for our dogs. For now, let's just acknowledge and learn from the love of Argos for Odysseus. He waits twenty years to see his human again. Then after remaining on watch for all those years, Argos sees Odysseus return home alive, and he can finally die in peace.

Our dogs love us. It is not unconditional love (I don't believe that exists), but with a bit of kindness, time, and care, they love us in return.

The other lesson here is that Homer, writing in 725 BCE, recognized the love a dog could have for a human. Think of that! For thousands of years, and long before Homer, dogs have loved us.

The next time your dog looks up at you with those dark brown eyes — or blue, or both; Oso, a Bernese mountain dog, had one blue eye and one brown eye — know there is a lot in that gaze. Thousands of years of moving from being wary, to depending on, to trusting, and then to loving. Now we are bound up, each in orbit around the other. What a gift it is to be loved by a dog.

Part 1

First Dog

*If having a soul means being able to feel love
and loyalty and gratitude,
then animals are better off than a lot of humans.*

— James Herriot, *All Creatures Great and Small*

When you are young, say ten, and your first dog joins the family, it is like starting an entirely new life. When it is a puppy, with puppy breath, puppy energy, there are no words that a normal ten-year-old has to describe how their life changes.

For our family it began when we moved from the suburbs of Minneapolis, where we were dogless, out to a dilapidated old summerhouse in the country that had been built in the 1930s. At that time, there were seven of us, five kids and two "grown-up" parents. I put *grown-up* in quotes because our dad had just turned twenty-nine and our mom was just twenty-seven.

They were in over their heads.

I didn't want to leave our suburban home. St. Louis Park was a great neighborhood. I had lots of friends and a crush on a certain girl. We would play capture the flag until dark. We'd chase the DDT truck down our street while running in and out of the cloud of toxins. (The motto: Better living through chemistry.) But our dad had become so involved in Minnesota politics and the civil defense force that his work was suffering. The big political issue in Minnesota was whether to remove the tax on margarine, which was fiercely battled by Minnesota butter producers. His civil defense job was to help with traffic in case of a nuclear attack. It was bucolic and dystopian all at once.

So we escaped to this place that, my dad eternally quipped, "wasn't the end of the world, but you could see it from there." Dad joke. For thirty years we'd all roll our eyes.

The house came with an overgrown pasture and twenty acres of woodland on the Minnesota River. The house had a cranky furnace, seriously Rube Goldberg plumbing, and air conditioning that occasionally worked. Giant bull snakes moved in and out, and squirrels and the occasional raccoon nested in the attic.

Kid heaven.

Our dad traveled a lot, leaving our mom in charge of five children under the age of ten in this quirky house at the end of a long, pitch-black-at-night dirt road. Although our mom loved it, I think she also felt a bit nervous about keeping us safe. Thus, the moment came, in 1961, when she told me, as the oldest, that we should get a dog.

There are joyous moments in every life. First kiss. (Thank you, Cindy Rose!) Graduating from high school and college. Getting married. Having kids. I rank picking out your first dog in the top five.

... And She Threw Up on My Shoes

I was excited and nervous on the way out.

My parents had friends from the old neighborhood who had decided to be farmers (a pro-butter family), escape the potential of a nuclear attack, and raise German shepherds. When we got to their farm, the dog guardian, whose name was Claire, after some chatter with my mom (a chat that took way too long for my state of excitement), asked me if I wanted to see the litter.

To that day, my encounters with dogs had been limited. There were the two Great Danes that lived in our old neighborhood. In the afternoon, their "mom" would call all the moms on the block and let them know that she was letting her dogs out for a run. We'd go in the house and the two huge Danes would sprint a couple of times up and down the block and then go home and we'd get the "all clear." (It was a different time.) Then, when I was seven, waiting for the school bus, I was attacked by two different dogs from across the street. Their entire family sprinted out the door to save me, and it did leave a touch of fear of dogs in my psyche.

All that was going on in my mind as I slowly got out of our family station wagon and followed my mom and Claire toward the barn.

The German shepherd mom came out, giving us the once-over. With her guardian there, she was friendly. I was instructed to put my hand out so she could smell it. Tentatively, I reached my arm out, she sniffed it, then she went up and did the same with my mom. We passed the first test.

We walked into the gloom of the barn, which smelled of fresh-cut hay, and I could hear the barking, yipping, and whining of multiple puppies.

I had never heard a puppy bark before.

There were about eight of them, all tumbling or resting in a paddock covered with straw. I must have been a little reticent because I remember Claire asking me if I wanted to go in the paddock and meet the puppies. Later, when our dogs had puppies, it became a family contest to see who could dive into the litter and be swarmed.

I nodded and Claire opened the paddock door. I walked in and was overwhelmed with German shepherd puppies: a wriggling, licking, nibbling, jumping-up mass of ten-week-old dogs. I sat down and they were all over me. I was petting, rubbing stomachs, and pushing away the puppies who wanted to lick my face.

Claire had already picked out a beautiful female for us, but in that moment, I wanted all of them.

This day was my first experience of the joy dogs bring. It is imprinted on my brain as if it just happened.

Riding home in the front seat, with the as-yet-unnamed puppy, I was more than a little overwhelmed. On the one hand, I was now responsible for this living creature (my dad was explicit, as all parents are, about that). On the other hand, as I held the puppy in my lap and she licked my hand, I was amazed. I couldn't stop smiling.

We had a dog!

It is important to stress that our family knew nothing about dogs. We just brought this puppy home without so much as a clue about what to do. Much like when you have your first child, the nurses get you ready to go home and you're stunned that they don't give you an instruction manual (*How to Raise Children from 0 to 18*).

My mom never had a dog. My dad's family had a dog, yet he was fuzzy on the details of raising a dog. His excuse was that he had been a socially busy teenager. Much of his fatherly input was done while he was on the road, via phone. When asked about specific things, like how to stop a puppy from pooping in the house, he'd usually say, "Love you! You'll figure it out. Gotta go!"

Our mom eventually got a book, and one of the first things we looked up was the pooping-in-the-house question. That's when we first discovered the concept of house-training. Imagine our mom and me smacking our foreheads at the same time: "House-training!"

My dad's family dog, a black Lab, was named Bonnie. This is an important detail because my parents, in an act of parental mischief, named one of my sisters after said Labrador. I thought at the time that it was kind of an honor. My sister, however, when she was old enough to make the connection, was not amused.

As we drove down our road, I put our puppy (I was so excited to think *our puppy*!) on the floor of the car. She promptly threw up on my shoes. I remember being shocked and grossed out. My mom, veteran of seven pregnancies and five babies, just smiled and told me I'd get over it. This is a major truth, a fact of life, but not one as a preteen I was ready to hear.

Of course, with our new dog, the first bit of business — after introductions to my four sisters, decisions on where the puppy should sleep, and who she *really* liked best — was to come up with a name.

This entailed much political lobbying, asking in favors, and some whining until as a family we voted. My dad constantly reminded us that our family was not a democracy, thus the parents got three votes each, were allowed to bribe one or two "weak" children, and tended to vote in a block. I had nominated the name Dog, which was my ten-year-old-boy idea of hilarity. My sister Bonnie had opted for Annie, our mom's name, which was her idea of retribution. My dad's friend and the neighborhood godfather, Bob Brown, suggested Touser. That is what he called all dogs. At the time I didn't know the most important rule of dog naming is to pick a name and then go to the backyard and yell the name three times as loud as you can. This usually eliminates possible names like Poukie or Roger that sound ridiculous when shouted. Simply picture yourself mortally embarrassed standing outside in your jammies at 7 a.m. begging your dog to come in as your neighbors look at you quizzically. Seriously, go yell "Poukie" a couple of times.

Our parents prevailed in the vote and our first dog was named Shawnee. A black-and-tan, pointy-eared German shepherd who soon ran the household.

Getting Over Poop

My daughter Brynne told me an important marker of a healthy, loving, and growing relationship is when you can freely talk about poop, pee, and vomit. Of course — and I would never say this to her face — in this area she is in the wisest class of folks, as a wife, mother, and doctor. The language of bodily fluids just rolls off her tongue.

For many individuals (mostly men), having children is their introduction to using the language of defecation out loud, for instance, the first time they find themselves yelling, "The baby pooped on me!"

Having a dog early in life is enormously helpful assistance for getting over the anxiety and embarrassment about excrement, and so on. This step is as important to our maturation as getting our first job.

Shawnee, for example, was my introduction to fifty years of dogs vomiting, pooping, and often peeing at the most inopportune times and places. Once when I brought a potential girlfriend home, Shawnee, sitting on the couch with us, farted.

I wanted to die.

At first, when asked to clean up poop, I reacted as if I was being told to climb down into our septic tank. Interestingly, my dad also responded rather badly when he was asked to pick up after the dogs.

It has been the women in my life — mom, wife, and

daughters — who in ways subtle and direct have helped me get over this aversion. I can now proudly affirm that I can talk, in public, about all of this, um, crap.

Here are more concrete lessons I've learned about poopology.

1. Poop, vomit, and pee happen. Clean it up and move on.
2. Make sure your children (and recalcitrant adults) read *Everyone Poops* by Taro Gomi.
3. Pick up your dog's poop. Please. Seriously. There are no poop-fairies who come at night and clean up after you and your dog. And don't leave the bags of poop on a trail thinking that the forestry folks will pick them up. It's not their job.
4. The time will come when the best house-trained dog, your dog, will look you in the eyes and then proceed to poop or pee in front of you, in your house. Breathe. Do not lose your cool. This too shall pass.

Although it is freeing to be able to talk about all the above, don't go overboard talking about your dog's defecation issues. Lots of people are not that liberated.

Save the Puppies!

The first year was as you would suspect: fun, messy, and chaotic. Kids and a dog chasing each other down hallways and in the pasture. Poop and pee in the house. Dad and Mom yelling at someone to clean it up! House-training theoretically made sense, but execution seemed out of our grasp.

Mostly we just let Shawnee do what she wanted to do. She had the run of the land; she slept in our beds on a rotating schedule, to be fair, and was treated like another kid. She just ate different food and had to poop outside (most of the time...). We didn't spay (desex) her because I don't think my parents knew what that meant. In their defense, they were staring down the barrel of two soon-to-be-sullen preteens and three rebellious daughters. They were mostly exhausted.

At six months, someone had the appropriate idea of taking Shawnee to puppy school. I was elected as the trainer. It did not go well. Apparently, at eleven, I wasn't "strong enough" to manage an extremely active and protective German shepherd. That rebuke ended in me doing lots of push-ups in our garage. (Ironically, fifty years later, our eighty-pound rescue Great Pyrenees took off on our first walk, sending me flying horizontally behind him, and my wife, Laurie, said essentially the same thing.)

Of course, having an unspayed female dog loose in the

country had unintended consequences. Predictable consequences, obviously, but none of us kids knew anything about
dog reproductive biology.

All we knew was that one day Shawnee was pregnant.
In the minds of Catholic youth, why not an immaculate dog
conception?

When our mom figured out that her "baby" was pregnant, she was indignant. She sat us down and, like the pros-
ecuting attorney that all moms can summon when needed,
asked us to report if anything had happened with Shawnee
when we were with her.

With excellent cross-examination skills, she drew the
story out of us.

The deed had happened on a summer afternoon. There
were a bunch of us, including my sisters and our closest
neighbors. Two of the neighbor girls and I were, as mentioned, inching toward puberty. Accompanying us was
Shawnee — she never left our sides when we were out and
about — and our neighbor's male collie-shepherd mix. As
it was most days, we were kids on the loose, with no adult
available to interpret the life-altering event we were about
to witness.

I won't go into the details of dog sex. Just let me say that
my little sister Patty was horrified that Buster, the neighbor's dog, was "attacking" Shawnee. Allan, the oldest and
most sophisticated at thirteen, just told us to leave them
alone. And the two neighbor girls and I never made eye
contact again once we simultaneously figured out what was
going on.

Our mom put all these facts together, read about dog

gestation in her new how-to book, calculated the timeline, chose not to pick this moment to explain sex to curious kids (how Action A leads to Reaction B), and began to watch Shawnee more closely.

Nine weeks later Shawnee disappeared one night. We called and called her but to no avail. My mom finally organized us with flashlights — by then she knew that Shawnee was no doubt delivering her puppies somewhere nearby. We searched until Shawnee appeared, thin and covered in sand, and went to the house and her food bowl. She ate voraciously and then scratched to get out. This time we followed her to an old badger den on the bluff. We could hear the muffled sounds of the pups as Shawnee slithered down into the hole.

A parental edict was announced over the objections of the gathered. "The puppies are fine. Shawnee knows what to do. We'll take care of them tomorrow. She'll probably bring them out herself. Everyone, to bed!"

Patty, sister number three, wanted to stay by the den and sleep outside, but she was overruled.

And the next day it rained.

Late that afternoon, as the rain continued, everyone was worried. Even though she was just seven, Patty was the dog (and animal) whisperer among us. Finally, she convinced our more laissez-faire mom that we needed to act.

As I was told later, it was decided that Patty should try to duck into the hole and see if she could grab the puppies. She got as far as her waist and then backed out, covered in mud. The den twisted at the end and was too small for Patty to reach.

Soaking wet, my sisters and our mom contemplated what to do next.

Then my mom shouted over the wind, "We can tie a rope around Peggy's waist. Then she can crawl into the den and pull the puppies out." Peggy was the youngest — five — and even then the bravest of us all. Peggy was drafted, *by her mom*, to try it next.

They were standing on a high bluff overlooking the Minnesota River. It was steep and sandy, and rain was pouring into the den.

Peggy was excited to try. With the rope looped around her waist, she began crawling headfirst down the passage.

It was 1963, and in rural Minnesota, it was not uncommon for individuals to put unwanted puppies in a sack and toss them in the river.

Thus, the idea of sending a five-year-old down a badger den to rescue five mixed-breed puppies…well, once that story got told, it raised eyebrows among the primarily Scandinavian- and German-descendant farmers in our new town. A raised eyebrow being a significant display of emotion.

As Peggy disappeared down the hole, my mother was beseeching the Norse gods and Indigenous spirits. (Mom's motto: Worship the local gods.) Patty was shining a flashlight down the tunnel to help, but soon Peggy was out of sight. Minutes passed. Then Peggy came crawling backward out of the hole, clutching a puppy. She handed it to Patty, who sprinted to the house and the bed we had built for the litter. Four more times, in the driving rain, Peggy crawled down and brought puppies back. Jubilant but soaked and covered in wet Minnesota sand, they finally retreated to the house.

An hour later, after hot showers and clean clothes, all of us gathered around the litter. In her new role as a mom, Shawnee was cleaning the puppies and feeding them.

Of course, as children, we were operating under the assumption that they were *our* dogs, and we immediately began naming the puppies. Our parents, however, put their foot down. We would keep no puppies. This led to a split in our family: emotional youth versus logical, rational parents.

"Free Love"

My sister Patty's vision was to keep all of them. A pasture alive with dogs. Every night, every bed with a puppy — or two — in it.

She brushed off "details" like the amount of poop there would be or the cost in food and vet care, not to mention what our neighbors would think about a platoon of dogs barking in unison at every living or moving thing.

The idea of having multiple dogs gave my dad nightmares. Where my sister Patty saw this idyllic pasture full of romping dogs, my dad saw his entire life spent chasing German shepherds as they chased cars, endlessly calling them to come in, swearing at them as they shook off mud and water in the living room, and ultimately being reduced to tears while he pleaded with them to get their muddy butts out of his car so he could go to work.

Our parents understood we needed to sell or give away the puppies within the small window of time after the puppies were weened and before their children became so attached that they would hide them in closets and under beds and blankets whenever humans came by to look at them for adoption.

Once the edict came down, the next divisive issue was who could take "our" puppies. Everyone wanted a say and threatened a veto if they were not heard. It was the sixties, and the power of feminism was emerging. In our house that meant that my dad and I were outnumbered five to two (six to two if you counted Shawnee). Since I was mostly terrified of my sisters, I tended to abstain or just stay in my room. Thus daughter-power ruled. From the girls, common objections were that the individuals didn't have kids, they lived too far away, or they lived in the city. If a man wore a hat, that was an automatic "no deal." I still don't understand why. If Shawnee growled, it was game over. The most common objection was just the sense that "it didn't feel right."

My father thought he'd raised his kids with the ideals of capitalism, that they knew the golden rule was never say no to a buyer with cash in hand, but he found he was up against a cabal of nonprofit idealists.

The Horror.

Watching our parents try to be autocratic was, however, laughable. They just didn't have the heart. Maybe it was because they had lost two children; maybe because they had both come from troubled homes. Or maybe, both being young, they just were not the "do what I say!" kind of grown-ups.

Negotiations commenced. My father agreed to eventually keep one puppy from one of Shawnee's litters (we knew more were coming). Patty, as the seven-year-old attorney representing the rest of us, agreed to let go of the "German shepherd farm" idea.

My dad agreed to the demands about good family homes for the rest of the puppies (but no one in hats!), and the kids agreed to help rather than actively or passive-aggressively resist every time someone came to see them.

Next, we all agreed to support his marketing plan. He put an ad in the paper with the headline: "Free Love!"

At first glance, in the staid Minneapolis *Star and Tribune*, some eyebrows were again raised, but the rest of the text read: "Ten-week-old German shepherd mix puppies. Mom is a German shepherd. Father is from a good neighborhood. Family dogs only!" Then our phone number.

There were often tears as we passed puppies into the arms of other children. And there was also this emerging sense that we were doing the right thing. We were, like the ad said, giving "love" away.

The puppies, as puppies do, played their part. It is a neat evolutionary trick. Dogs evolved to appeal to our sense of "cuteness," and we evolved to be drawn to cuteness. In 1943, Austrian ethologist and zoologist Konrad Lorenz named this "cuteness" the "baby schema." Flatter faces, chubby round bodies, floppy ears, lots of eye contact. Dogs, as compared to wolves of the same age, are more approachable, docile, and subservient, and they hold on to puppy-like traits long into dog-hood. Scientists call this *neoteny*, holding childlike characteristics into adulthood.

As a child, what I wondered about was how Shawnee felt about her offspring leaving. Maybe she desired that pasture full of her pups. On the other hand, being constantly chased by her brood, even after they were weaned, must have been exhausting. Our mom, who had just had another baby boy, Joey, was especially sympathetic to that point of view. And even with later litters, after the puppies reached ten weeks or so, Shawnee seemed blasé about the whole maternal instinct thing. She was content to get back to her routine of napping (alone) on the porch.

The Legacy of Little Joe

Three issues confounded Shawnee's desire to, like most moms, have a little peace. First, she was a "free" dog, able to roam wherever she wanted. That led to all sorts of encounters with male dogs, one specifically that we'll get to in a moment.

Second, even after that first litter, she wasn't desexed. Surgically removing sex organs from dogs was relatively unpracticed in the 1960s and 1970s. As dog populations increased, this led to a catastrophic increase in unwanted animals. In 1970, one shelter in Eugene, Oregon, was receiving up to one hundred dogs a day. (At the time, animal control was not even bringing cats to shelters.) Most of those dogs were euthanized. By 2015, after spaying was introduced as a general practice, the same shelter reported that intakes had dropped to less than 10 percent of that number.

We didn't have a dog spayed until the late seventies.

Third, there was this specific male dog, my dad's nemesis, Little Joe.

One of the great pleasures of growing up was watching my dad, in a shirt, tie, boxer shorts, and dark socks, chasing Little Joe out of our house in the mornings. Not every morning, but frequently and regularly enough to suspect that "Little Joe" had an accomplice.

Little Joe was a farm dog, a loosely-attached-to-the-neighborhood dog. He was a border collie mix and all unneutered male. In retrospect, he was probably the father of more litters in our community than any other dog. He was our community's Genghis Khan.

The best part of these mornings was when Dad, out of breath from chasing, and wondering what had happened to his life, bellowed to the household that he wanted a family meeting *right now*!

Sleepy children wandered from the bedrooms and assembled in front of him: three little girls still clutching teddy bears and two preteens.

A side note: My father was a highly successful entrepreneur and speaker. He was accustomed to the risks and challenges of the business world. He was beloved by the individuals who worked for him. And standing in front of us, wearing, as I mentioned, a shirt, tie, and boxer shorts, and especially those black socks and dress shoes, he lacked a certain authority.

And he knew, deep in his heart, not only were these difficult conversations, but that each ultimately would fail. First, because he was not the holder of power and justice; in other words, he was not the mom. Second, because he was up against his antagonist, my sister Patty.

In our family, Patty was the lover and protector of all things four-legged or winged. This meant dogs, horses, and our resident crow named Star. My grandmother Cici, who lived with us during the summers, believed that Star was her long-departed sister Gladys, visiting her from heaven. (I'm fairly certain that belief wasn't sanctioned by the church, but Cici always went her own way.) Then there was Penelope, the pig. Penelope caused the ultimate break between my sister and my dad. When Penelope was sent to the "farm up north," it took Patty only a day to figure out what had really happened. She then busted our dad, telling him that if he ever had bacon in our house again, she'd throw it in his face.

She could be scary that way.

Patty litigated for the raccoons that got into our dishwasher and the squirrels in the attic.

Regarding Little Joe, imprinted in my brain are conversations like this:

My dad, calmly at first: "Did someone let Little Joe into the house?"

Silence, except for some sniffling.

Then, a touch of despair in his voice, my dad asking, "Patty?"

And Patty, her exasperated tone directed at the rest of us to remind us how hard it was to explain anything important to a grown-up, saying, "Dad, Little Joe and Shawnee are married. He just wanted to be with her."

Unassailable logic.

And our mom, holding Joey, would summon all her powers to stifle a laugh.

I could see my dad, once named the "world's greatest salesman" by *The Today Show*, trying to stay calm and think of persuasive arguments. I could see Patty — who was noted for this — marshaling her arguments into bullet points to counter any attempt at emotional pleading.

My sister Bonnie — playing the part of the rebellious almost teenager — might utter some monosyllabic groan and head back upstairs as our mom told the rest of us to get ready for school, which left our dad and Shawnee in the hallway looking at each other.

Of course, Little Joe got off scot-free. I'd see him scrunch under the barbwire fence and trot across the pasture toward wherever he called home. No doubt to a dog dish of food by a barn and a victory nap on a porch.

Little Joe was an approachable and friendly dog. He apparently had no serious responsibilities: He was free.

As a fifth grader in Sister Mildred's class, I often day-dreamed about what that meant, to be free. To have every day in front of you and do anything you wished. To not be accountable — which was apparently Little Joe's case — to anyone. To wander, tramp, circle back, chase down smells, run with a group of boys (and my sister Susie) playing touch football. And then to drop down wherever you were and take a nap, panting and resting your head on your paws.

I idolized Little Joe. Over the few years when he was a

regular at our house — I'm sure he was being secretly fed and pampered by my sisters and possibly our mom — our kid lives slowly began to emulate his. We were making the transition from suburban children to country kids or, as our mom and dad would opine, to wild animals. In the summers, released from the confines of Catholic school, we quickly descended into woodland animists. My dad would come home from a week on the road and be aghast at his children. He'd find us all in one room, Shawnee in the middle, and hear chilling stories of bull snakes wrapped around pipes in the basement, of our pet crow stealing jewelry, of Patty's latest attempt to feed raccoons, and of me being chased by a rabid fox. I'd see him look at my mom, who loved our summers, and send her telepathic messages: *Are these uneducated heathens going to live with us forever?*

And of course, I thought the answer was yes. As in many families, there were darker times ahead, but then I was sure I had the perfect life.

If you are a grown-up reading this, with a job, family, responsibilities, *a list* of tasks, unwind and remember what it was like to be twelve. To get up in the morning — to want to get up — and throw on jeans, a T-shirt, and sneakers, then inspect your insect collection, grab something to eat, say goodbye to your parents, and go outside with a dog with the intention of not coming back until lunch or maybe dinner. No money, no iPhone, just a dog, some snacks, and on some days, a book or a fishing pole. Running not to get in shape but because it was the fastest way to get somewhere. The magic of your first bike. All this before puberty (the Great Interrupter), before "knowing things" took the place of wonder, before status and being "cool" became the dominate motivators.

Free. Wanderers. Trampers. The clarity of being a twelve-year-old hanging out with a dog.

Freedom

——— ∞ ———

Freedom: The absence of necessity, coercion,
or constraint in choice, action, or thought.

At the end of *Adventures of Huckleberry Finn*, Huck says, "But I reckon I got to light out for the territory ahead of the rest, because Aunt Sally she's going to adopt me and sivilize me and I can't stand it. I been there before."

Every time I've watched one of our dogs get out a door or jump a fence, I think they want to "light out for the territory." Not all dogs. Maisie, our Chihuahua-terrier mix, is content to be always in the house with us. Her history suggests that she was lost and by herself for quite a while as a puppy.

Most of our other dogs have been "escape artists." Underneath the door opening, jumping, and digging. There seems to be an innate desire to escape being trapped in a house or a fenced yard.

Of course, the reason we have fenced yards, or keep our dogs in the house or a crate, and keep them on leashes on walks or runs, is to keep them "safe." We don't want them to get lost (they can be lousy navigators, as mentioned), get into a fight with another dog, or hit by a car. There are real and often tragic consequences for a "gone" dog.

To be sure, I am an advocate of fences, locks on doors, and sadly, even leashes. I want our dogs safe.

And every time I've watched one of our dogs defeat our best attempts to keep them fenced in, every time they take off, something gnaws at me. This is true even as I run after them, leash in hand, to catch them.

It is the dynamic between freedom and safety, between adventure and playing it safe. A dog gets out, takes off, and is gone for hours. They come back, tired, panting, and thirsty. When that happens, I'm overjoyed that they are back and safe — and I immediately try to figure out how to fix the fence. I also wonder, what did they see or smell? What kind of adventure did they have?

It is hard truth that when we "light out for the territory," or go on an adventure (that is, any endeavor where the outcome is uncertain), we by necessity need to give up a bit of safety. I don't think dogs do this kind of calculus. We, on the other hand, as overthinkers, are often caught in this problem: *Shall I go for it, or shall I stay inside my fence? Do I want to be constrained, or do I want to be my true, free self?*

Although we can never really know, watching a dog think as they observe a fence is a wonderful metaphor for our personal question. Safety or adventure? Light out for the territory or stay on the couch?

I tend to side with Helen Keller, who said: "Security is mostly a superstition. It does not exist in nature.... Avoiding danger is no safer in the long run than outright exposure. Life is either a daring adventure, or nothing."

WILDNESS

Now I see the secret of making the best persons.
It is to grow in the open air and to eat and sleep with the earth.

— WALT WHITMAN

As promised — cross my heart, hope to die — we kept one of Shawnee's puppies from her second litter. Following the tradition of ill-advised names, we named her Rikka after a friend of my then-girlfriend. Of course, that did not go over well with her, but we loved the name.

When Rikka was six months old, she joined Shawnee and me, and we used our freedom to explore the Big Woods.

Before the arrival of Europeans, in the time of the Dakotas, over 60 percent (30 million acres) of Minnesota was covered by forests. Long gone now, cleared for farmland, lumbered for cities back east, burned in fires (some of the most horrific wildfires in the early part of the twentieth century were in Minnesota and Wisconsin), these forests were called the Big Woods, ancient forests with trees so large and dense that sunlight barely reached the forest floor.

Our house was perched on a windswept bluff (think the Yorkshire moors and the Brontë sisters) overlooking some of the remaining forests, the bottomland of the Minnesota River valley.

The first time I dove into the woods was following Shawnee. I was trepidatious at first, counterpoint to Shawnee's desire to get out and go.

The bluffs by our house were steep. As Shawnee, and later Rikka, plunged down them, I slowly followed, picking a trail, going sideways, being careful.

The dogs' ears were always up. They'd zigzag back and forth trying to pick up scents from the rich bottomland of the Minnesota River. I'd trail behind, picking my way through "itch-weed," climbing over dead trees, and avoiding poison ivy.

After a few months of learning to trust the dogs and being at home in the woods, it became who we were, what we did: a boy, two dogs, and the river valley.

The wide and flat valley of the Minnesota is what is left after cataclysmic events that happened twelve thousand years or so ago. During the last glacial period, at the end of the Last Glacial Maximum, the north country (from coast to coast and as far south as Illinois) was covered by almost a mile-high sheet of ice. Think the ice wall in *Game of Thrones*, but much, much higher. The seas were four hundred feet lower than today. For our Northern Hemisphere ancestors — and their dogs — the wall of ice that dominated the horizon to the north must have been one of the most epic challenges humans ever faced.

In states like Minnesota, the glaciers were such a monumental part of prehistory that geologically we can still note their impact. For example, the north country is "rebounding" from those glaciers at about one centimeter a year. It's theorized that the rebounding will continue for the next ten thousand years. The earth is always in motion.

The Minnesota River valley was formed by the outflow of Lake Agassiz — a giant glacial lake that covered much of northwest Minnesota, North Dakota, and parts of Canada.

It is believed the outflow was caused by catastrophic events. For example, the collapse of glacial ice dams, or the rebound of the earth after the glaciers retreated. I imagine a churning wall of water, tearing southward, carving, carving as it went, pushing boulders, trees, creating a brand-new landscape. The outflow was so large, moving through the River Warren to the ancient Mississippi and north to Hudson Bay, that it alone raised sea levels over three feet.

My mom, an amateur historian of all things having to do with the Minnesota River, made sure that I knew all this. She would read and tell me about the land we stood on, the history of the Indigenous people (the First People), the coming of the Germans and Scandinavians, the wildlife and trees. And the bugs, you cannot forget the bugs: clouds of mosquitoes, deer flies, horse flies, and ticks that swell until they are bulbous and gray.

Understanding where we stood, and who had stood there before, was the tuition she charged for freeing a thirteen-year-old with our dogs to dive down the river-deposited sandy bluffs, through the tall grass, back a thousand years, and into the woods.

As in every wild place, the banks of the Minnesota were full of science. The artifacts of thousands of years of floods, winters, and fires slept in the clay soil under us.

But unlike scientists, as children in the woods, we didn't have the domains of knowledge. A botanist studies plants; a freshwater biologist can explain in detail the fish that thrive in the river and lake turnover. A geologist can tell stories of the great Lake Agassiz floods. But a young teen with his dogs, sitting on a gray bank, watching rotting trees tumble and flow by in the river, seeing turtles pop their heads up in the current, can only experience the Great Oneness of the wild. If you open yourself up to that experience, not only is the natural world laid bare, everything you need to know about life, morality, and consequence is before you.

Wildness in all its richness teaches, if we pay attention. And in the woods, there is no guide better for paying attention and noticing than a dog.

Once, we came across a deer that had died a few days prior. Its corpse had been torn open by the abundant variety of opportunistic animals, nocturnal and otherwise, bacterial and carnivore.

I held both dogs away from the rotting body and stared at what remained of the deer. I thought about death. Although we still prefer not to think about death and dying in our culture, in the wild its presence is ubiquitous.

My grandfather, who had been my mentor of all things in the woods and lakes, had recently passed away. We had fished and hunted together since I was six. He was a World War I veteran and ex-Kentuckian bootlegger. We squirrel hunted together, and his favorite thing was to shoot a red squirrel out of a tree in such a way that it would land on me. He was that good of a shot. He taught me how to clean, grill, and eat squirrel, much to the dismay of my mom and the disgust of my sisters. And yes, what little meat there was tasted like chicken. (I learned that if there were squirrels, I could survive in the woods.)

We had been scheduled to go on a fishing trip with his

fishing buddies, but at the last minute I canceled, as I had a potential girlfriend I wanted to see instead. Puberty hit just like that.

My grandfather, in his sleep that Saturday night, in the same motel we were supposed to stay in together, had a massive heart attack and died. He was sixty-five.

There was a funeral, and being Catholic, it was an open casket. Walking in procession up to the casket, I noticed that he looked peaceful and clean. I was heartbroken and felt terribly guilty. But it didn't feel real. And the religiosity of it, the discussion of an unseeable soul ("I have said that the soul is not more than the body," Whitman wrote), an unknowable God, this place called heaven, and the solace that somewhere my grandfather still existed — all of that made no sense to me.

The wilderness teaches a different lesson. On that summer day standing in the mud of the valley, staring at the deer, I thought, *This is true death*. A vibrant animal, now fallen, now returning to dust, soon to disappear. As is nature's way, nothing is wasted. Food for animals and insects and microorganisms, that they may live another day.

I had no idea what Shawnee and Rikka thought about a dead deer. I doubt they wondered about theological implications. Mostly, they both wanted to roll in the carcass for unknown dog reasons.

Here is where our fear of anthropomorphizing gets in the way. We have been trained to think that, when an animal looks upon death, they must not be even *thinking*. Or best case, they are thinking no more than *food* or *intense smell*.

I wonder. Decades later, I was driving up a switchback

road in the mountains above Santa Fe. Winding around a corner, I came upon a deer lying on its side on the road. I pulled over, walked over, and felt it. It was still warm, but dead. It must have just been hit by a car. Standing on the other side of the road were two does. They were staring at their dead companion and me. I have no idea what they were thinking.

Yet the fact that they stayed there, seemingly unafraid of me, and just gazed upon death struck me that something else was going on in their heads, even if it was just the immediate shock of "now you're here, now you're not" — when death happens suddenly. I think the most honest answer is we don't know. I don't want my curiosity to be limited by anthropocentric thinking.

Multiple summers, autumns, winters when the river and the swamps froze over, and springs when the ice broke up and boomed day and night, the three of us spent our days in the river bottoms. School was an often unpleasant and boring interruption to my real education, the teachings of the woods.

More than once sitting on the riverbank, with Shawnee lounging beside me, and the puppy Rikka rooting around in the dirt, I had this sense that this was the most important place to be. I had not then the vocabulary to express it, just the sense that it was more sacred, to use that lovely word, than serving mass in our small-town Catholic church, which I still faithfully did each Sunday.

Being by the river with dogs, whom I loved, was more vital to me than being with the pomposity of grown-ups speaking confusing and archaic language, be it Catholic, Christian, or Buddhist.

I sat there with these bright-eyed, curious, and sentient beings. If I lay back and closed my eyes, I could imagine the roaring of the first waters of the River Warren, feel the awe that must have inspired in the Indigenous people who witnessed it twelve thousand years ago.

Shawnee, our first family dog, led me here. Maybe not with some grand scheme in mind. Possibly because being in the wilderness with one of her humans was for her the best of all possible worlds.

For me, however, this became bedrock, the foundation of how I wanted to live. If I wandered too far away from Woods, River, Dog — which I have — I felt adrift. There are days, even now, especially now, where I feel disconnected, not sure where I fit, then I remember.

Woods, River, Dog.

I know this seems highfalutin. Yet sitting on the bank of the Minnesota, in that ancient valley, with Shawnee's head on my lap, it was clear, it was simple.

When we adopted Shawnee, I thought only of how cool it was to be with and to love a dog. In our last years together, before going away to college and joining "the world," as all that change of life swirled around, Shawnee became my touchstone. She was my reminder that no matter what, whether I left and came back, failed at college, was dumped by a girl, I could always shed my skin and we could dive down the bluffs again, run along the banks and be wild together. Woods, River, Dog.

I have an old Kodak film picture of Shawnee standing on the banks of the river looking out over what I'm sure she thought of as her domain. I've carried it with me for fifty years, in my trunk when I've traveled and in boxes when we've moved. It's now pinned to a bulletin board in our home office.

She was the first dog. She passed while I was at school. That is just the way with dogs and us. And the lesson still lives with me: Woods, River, Dog.

DOG LESSON

Wild at Heart

꧁꧂

*I love even to see the domestic animals reassert their native
rights, any evidence that they have not wholly lost
their original wild habits and vigor; as when my neighbor's
cow breaks out of her pasture early in the spring and
boldly swims the river, a cold, gray tide, twenty-five or
thirty rods wide, swollen by the melted snow. It is the
buffalo crossing the Mississippi.*

— HENRY DAVID THOREAU

The word *domesticated* comes from the Latin *domus*, for "from the home." We think of domesticated as the antonym of wild. There are domesticated animals and plants, and there are their wild cousins.

With our current dogs, I'm fairly certain that if we dropped Maisie, our Chihuahua mix, into a wilderness, she probably would not fare well. (Maisie, we'd never do that!) Same for Toby, our Great Pyrenees, although he might have more of a fighting chance. Neither are adapted to nor have the skills to survive long term in the wild like their coyote and wolf relatives.

And yet…

In both our dogs, in your dog, like Thoreau's cow, there is wildness.

Wildness doesn't just mean the ability to live in the

wilderness. It is something deeper and more profound. For us (humans), it starts with the realization that we live in the natural world and are subject to its rules, whether we are dog, bacteria, or human. (As Covid reminded us.)

We have wild roots. We have instincts, needs, and behaviors that come from our deep history. We are not born blank slates. We are born with the instincts to survive in a small tribe in a wild world: They thrum in us.

Yet human culture strongly pushes back on our wildness. This goes as far back as Gilgamesh (possibly 2400 BCE). In this story, Enkidu, the wild man (symbolic of wildness and animal nature), is defeated by Gilgamesh and becomes a civil man.

Next, for those of us raised in a Judeo-Christian home, we have been taught (in Genesis 1:26) that we are separate and apart from nature: "Then God said, 'Let us make mankind in our image, in our likeness, so that they may rule over the fish in the sea and the birds in the sky, over the livestock and all the wild animals, and over all the creatures that move along the ground."

Finally, our language creates opposites: black or white, this or that, either-or, domesticated or wild. Nature, our biosphere, our web of life, is not that simple. It is messy, complicated, and full of surprises. Time and again we try to delineate human intelligence from animals, to hold on to the distinctions between our civilized selves and nature. Time and again those attempts go to ground. Chimpanzees and crows use tools. Whales sing. Leaf ants "domesticate" fungus. Honeybees practice and communicate navigational math. Bees play.

Yes, yes, of course, we are the most intelligent species on the planet. (Of course, we are the definer, judge, and jury of that claim.) We are civilized (mostly). And we are also wild. Thoreau's cow is a metaphor for this: a domesticated animal responding to that deep calling. We all have it; we need to listen to it.

Each time one of our dogs goes to "alert" on a walk, I am reminded of it. They move easily from sleeping on the couch to wild responses. They don't make the human distinction between domesticated or wild; they just live by their nature and experience. That's the lesson. To be fully human means not solely accepting the artifacts of civilization. It is also accepting our wild selves, to see us as part of the natural world.

When a Wild Place Disappears

Faeries, come take me out of this dull world,
For I would ride with you upon the wind,
Run on the top of the dishevelled tide,
And dance upon the mountains like a flame.

— William Butler Yeats

Everything ends, changes, transforms, or is swept away by glacial torrents. There is no constancy. Kids grow up, move on, come back, and then leave for good. Families explode. Divorces happen. Kids get married and start having children (and dogs) of their own. Sometimes, faithful to a place, trying to hold to the way things were, a dog lies on the porch of an empty home, waiting for children to return.

Having left home, gone to college, traveled, and worked for a while, I returned to Minnesota, fell in love, and got married to Laurie. We were married in a cold November, and we set up house with the first two of our own dogs, Riva, another German shepherd mix, and a lunatic collie named Nugie. She was named after my mom — her maiden name was Nugent — over her objections and to the delight of my sister Bonnie.

That winter, after a blizzard, we headed out to my family home in Minnesota.

There was three feet of new snow. The storm had built drifts on the bluffs that came up to my waist. As it is after a storm passes, it was bitterly cold.

I was wearing an orange puffy parka, Sorel boots, long underwear, and jeans.

I was out of breath, partially because I was post-holing through the snow — first tracks! — and because I was being chased by Riva and Nugie.

This was the kind of day that Northerner's dream about. It's the time before they worry about shoveling or driving. The city and countryside are shut down and silent. Roads snow-covered. Plans thrown out the window. Work stopped.

On days like this you huddle in your apartment or house, read seed catalogs, dream of spring and the veggie garden you'll plant come a warm April. Or, if you have whiny dogs, you head out into the snow.

I "ran" ten yards, collapsed, and was immediately jumped by the dogs. Then I got up and did it again and again.

Laurie followed our trail, calling us idiots, telling us that it was supposed to snow again, and if we got caught out here, there'd be a reckoning.

But we were in the zone where there was nothing else but snow-loving play.

And dogs smile! They barked with joy, they dove into banks of snow, disappearing. Their snouts were white with it. When tired, they just lay down where they were, tongues out, breathing the crisp postblizzard air.

We had a passion for snow. Growing up, our German shepherds were perfectly content burrowing into snowbanks and sleeping — until they were sure everyone in the house was asleep, and then they'd paw at the doors and whine to get in.

My mother's excitement with a coming storm was partly to blame. Her enthusiasm for a potential snow Armageddon and the joyous possibility of multiple snow days was infectious.

With our mom at the helm, in the days before a storm, the radio and TV were on constantly as the entire state went into a frenzy of preparation. No one could out-prepare our mom. Groceries bought. Bird feeders filled. Peanut butter and suet out on the railings. Propane tank filled, wood for fireplaces stacked.

She was propelled by two reasons. First, her amusement at the arrogance of civilization: believing that it could withstand anything that nature could throw at it. She loved the idea of the world being shut down, closed, immobilized by the weather. The howl of forty-mile-an-hour winds, zero visibility in blowing snow, followed by absolute silence the next morning was to her confirmation that nature was still in charge.

Then there was the incontestable beauty of the prairie after a storm, before there were tracks, before the town plows started clearing the roads. She'd be up at dawn, coffee in hand, dogs by her side, staring out the window at miles and miles of silence and white.

This was the hour of quiet before kids shuffled down for breakfast, our dad worked the phones canceling his day, and the dogs were up and aching to make first tracks.

Laurie's and my trip with our dogs that day was one of our final times making first tracks. What we didn't know was that under the snow, sleeping, were stakes, hundreds of them, marking out a housing development. The plan included hundreds of acres, the hills and swales, the creek that ran through it, and the stands of ancient trees.

Can a land whisper, *How could this happen?* Can trees bend in sadness, knowing that a hundred thousand years of their ancestors will be forgotten? It is heartbreaking when a wild place disappears. Thousands of years of topsoil converted into asphalt, whole ecosystems of grasses, trees, mammals, and insects wrenched from the planet.

Within a year, there were new roads. Within two, there were new houses, with dirt for front yards.

Five years later, it was one large commuter suburb with green and manicured lawns.

After my parents divorced and taxes skyrocketed, our mom had to sell our home. The buyer promptly sold it to a developer who tore it down. My room on the second floor: gone. The stand of white pine that sheltered our house from the winds: ripped from the ground. Our barn, the pasture: abolished from this earth. A lovely landscape turned into a dreamscape of a place that no longer exists.

Also during this time, I had my first experience of putting down a dog. Shawnee had died while I was in college. But Rikka, loyal Rikka, had stuck with our family through the "explosion," the selling of the house, and moving with my mom to a condominium.

But Rikka was sick. She was nine and arthritic. She could hardly get up, and she dragged her rear legs behind her when she tried to walk. She'd still lick our hands and beat her tail against the floor when we approached, but she was in pain.

It was up to me, the oldest at twenty-three, and I just didn't know what to do. One day I loaded her in the car and drove to the veterinarian. I had to carry her into the clinic. As was the custom then, I left her with the vet assistant, and then I walked away, got in my car, and cried. It was the hardest and dumbest thing I had done in my young life. Now, in my seventies, I cannot imagine leaving a dying dog alone to be put down. Then I was young and accepted the current "way." Stupid.

Our childhood world had ended, and Rikka along with it.

I often wonder, if Shawnee and Rikka could see what has become of their paradise, what would they think? From dirt roads to suburban streets. Forests to condos. And then there are these unrecognizable things called leashes.

They had never been leashed.

For me, this is the metaphor for what has happened — from unleashed to leashed. Now, as you walk those same acres, bisected into yards, asphalt, and houses, dogs are leashed by ordinance, by common agreement that it is safer for everyone, including the dogs.

If you have ever watched a dog sprint through an open field, chasing an uncatchable rabbit, sprinting back to you, and then just running because they can, you know how heartbreaking this is.

Some argue that this is growth (our American addiction). People need houses. Some believe, implicitly in their actions, if not explicitly in their words, that we are here to subjugate the wild. (My mother would laugh at this presumption.)

Mine may be a minority opinion, yet of equal weight are the muskrats being driven out and the pileated woodpeckers disappearing.

Of course, rural Minnesota is not the only place where this is happening. Driving west over the mountains of the Front Range, on a road I used to take as a college student, I once crested a hill expecting to see the endless and empty Great Plains. Instead, all I saw were houses from horizon to horizon.

Again, heartbreaking.

Ecologists and conservationists explain that this kind of "growth" can't go on forever. In the West, there are water restraints. *There is not enough water.* In the Midwest, there is the awful thought of the horizon disappearing: suburbs where there once was farmland. Shopping malls where there once were woods, swamps, and prairies.

But there are also spiritual reasons. In our deep cultural imagination, out "there" lies the wilderness. We may not ever visit (a shame …), yet we know it's there. Knowing that it is there, that there are wide-open, untrammeled mountains and prairies, rivers and coastlines, is a solace to our souls. There are still places to escape to, still places of dark skies, only starlight, and nobody for miles.

But what if they were gone? What if there were no parks, fields, pastures, hikes; places where you and your unleashed dog could just go? What if, horizon to horizon, there were just houses, buildings, roads, shopping centers, and manicured lawns? What if wilderness only existed in our imaginations and memories?

Who could live in that world?

My dream is that someday a developer will look at one hundred acres of old Minnesota prairie and think: *This is wild, and it's hallowed.* They'll see grasses, coneflowers, and black-eyed Susans. They'll hear the million-year-old sounds of insects and see the birds in flight and overhead a circling red-tailed hawk.

In their imagination, a dog, unleashed, running with joy, chased by children. And they'll think, *Yes, this is enough.*

Part 2

Philosophy of Dog

*Dogs are our link to paradise. They don't know evil
or jealousy or discontent. To sit with a dog on a hillside
on a glorious afternoon is to be back in Eden,
where doing nothing was not boring — it was peace.*

— Milan Kundera

If we go through our lives not stopping, not watching, not listening, not studying, we are doomed to live in a black-and-white world and miss the astonishing complexity, color, connectedness, contradictions, and beautiful fragility of our lives and world.

Case in point is how we "hold" dogs (and all animals, for that matter) in our lives.

We have a long and rich history with dogs. Some anthropologists even suggest that our ancient relationship with dogs was crucial to our survival as a species. That might be difficult to believe as you watch your shih tzu carry their favorite toy to the couch and burrow under pillows, but even shih tzus come from a long line of dogs who've kept us safe.

In this part, I want to deeply think about dogs and develop a philosophy, if you will, that most closely supports what we know and how we should treat our first nonhuman companions.

The Great Horned Owl

The past is never dead. It's not even past.

— William Faulkner

When Shawnee was still with us and eight years old, and I was in my late teens, we started running every morning in the summers. (Running in Minnesota's below-zero winter is not advised, yet true Minnesotans still do it.) She loved running with me, and even though I was often bleary-eyed in the early morning, I loved running with her.

One morning, we headed down an old dirt road. It was barely maintained and dropped down from our house, tunneling through the trees from the bluffs to the valley floor. It was 6:30 a.m. and twilight. The tops of the trees were beginning to glow green in the rising sun, and the forest floor and the road were a gloomy gray.

As we picked up our pace going downhill and I watched Shawnee run, two things happened simultaneously. First, I felt the hair on the back of my neck rise. I have no idea how that happened when I hadn't seen or heard anything. Second, Shawnee suddenly crouched, hackles up. This all happened in milliseconds. My brain short-circuited, logic and reason went out the door, and the limbic fight-flight-or-freeze brain kicked in. I ducked and froze. A dark shadow flew close to my head and soared over Shawnee. Then it was gone, into the deep woods. It was a great horned owl. Big — a five-foot wingspan — and silent in flight, deadly if you were a small mammal.

I felt like a small mammal. I felt hunted. I was back millions of years in the Paleocene. No longer an apex predator, but rather prey. No claws, no serious incisors — no plan to fight. I was alone, slow, and visible. I wondered for a second, what was I doing on an open road?

All my senses were on full alert. Shawnee, who had darted into the woods to escape, slowly came back and sat down next to me, panting.

That great owl awoke primordial senses, reminding me that I was animal first. *The past is never dead. It's not even past.* No matter how high in a skyscraper we live or work, no matter how distant we are from walking barefoot next to a lake or across the plains, we come from the ancient story of life on this planet, which began billions of years ago.

After a few moments of calming down, heartbeat back to normal, we got up and resumed our run. We moved out of the forest and onto the great flood plains of the Minnesota River, downriver from Shakopee. It's a migratory stop for waterfowl and teems with life. It was nirvana for Shawnee.

As she paced me, I thought about the encounter. Shawnee and I both shared a similar reaction to an unseen threat, exaggerated by the early-morning darkness and gloom. I didn't react any differently than Shawnee. I didn't stand straight up and think, *I will use my human big brain to analyze whether or not I'm in danger.* As an aside, nothing would get an early hominid eaten faster than that kind of "analysis paralysis." Rather, I ducked and, for that second or two, was adrenaline-flowing terrified.

Shawnee and I can both thank our evolutionary histories for our reactions, going as far back as our common ancestor, which existed anywhere from 100 million to 60 million years ago. Dogs and humans share approximately 84 percent of our genes. For some context, chimpanzees and humans share almost 98 percent of our genes. And as my daughter Sully has quipped, we are also 80 percent water, which basically makes us cucumbers with anxiety.

As mammals, we have a lot in common.

Dogs evolved from a now-extinct wolf species. Their closest living relative, the gray wolf, originated approximately a million years ago. In packs, gray wolves probably hunted the small hunter-gatherer families of *Homo sapiens*.

Then, forty to thirty thousand years ago something happened that changed everything.

We don't know what happened, though it's interesting to hypothesize. Maybe an enterprising hunter-gatherer took wolf pups from a den and began to "train" them. Maybe an enterprising wolf pack began to follow a clan and eat their scraps.

Or as some researchers theorize, maybe wolves evolved themselves, and the ones who were "friendlier" with humans changed into what we now recognize as dogs. This is the "survival of the friendliest" theory. The Russian scientist Dmitry Belyayev (1917–1985) worked with silver foxes to investigate this idea. In an astonishing project that has lasted over six decades, Dr. Belyayev and his team selected and bred silver foxes for "tameness." In each generation, the top 10 percent of the foxes considered the most "tame" were bred together. Over subsequent generations, not only did foxes become tamer (whining when humans left, wagging tails when humans returned), physical differences appeared: floppy ears, curly tails, lowered stress hormone levels, increased serotonin levels. They also had more juvenilized facial features, for example, shorter, more dog-like snouts.

The foxes were only bred for tameness, yet clearly the genes that controlled tameness also influenced physiological changes.

Possibly the same dynamic was at work with wolves and humans. As humans treated certain characteristics — like friendliness — preferentially, the wolves with those characteristics passed those traits, physical and behavioral, on to their offspring. And after enough generations, those offspring evolved into a new "domesticated" species, one specifically adapted to living with humans.

To sum up, a nascent relationship was born. Kind of like Bogart in *Casablanca* telling the French captain, "Louis, I think this is the beginning of a beautiful friendship."

Dogs became our first nonhuman partners.

How important was that relationship? Some scientists assert that it was a game changer in our path to modernity. One researcher, controversially, mused that *Homo sapiens* were able to outcompete Neanderthals in prehistoric Europe because they had dogs. Dogs were early warning partners when danger approached. They were a hunting partner, a garbage disposal, and probably a pack animal.

Dogs also learned to help herd and keep other domesticated animals safe. For example, our current dog, Toby, is a Great Pyrenees. That breed evolved in Asia Minor approximately ten thousand years ago, and they were probably brought to the Pyrenees mountains in France and Spain to stay with and protect sheep from wolves as far back as 3000 BCE. Now, with no sheep to protect, Toby spends a lot of time following me from room to room in our home.

Finally, dogs were probably a food source themselves for ancient peoples. In some countries, they still are.

The relationship between humans and dogs has also "grown" and evolved. We have adapted to optimally interact with dogs. Dr. Ádám Miklósi, of Eötvös Loránd University in Hungary, has studied barking. Wolves only bark to warn, while dogs have a much larger repertoire of barks. And guess what? In his study, humans were able to accurately tell the difference between at least six different barks, such as warnings, excitement, distress, and lonely barks. Over time, dogs and people have learned how to communicate with each other.

When we look at our dogs, we see this: a complex, social, bonding mammal — like us, devoted to us — who has been a significant factor in our survival as a species.

Thus, when you think about the puppy napping on your couch, or barking at the FedEx driver, remember that you are looking at nearly forty thousand years of coevolution.

Finally, as your dog rolls over for a belly rub, remember that maybe, back in the haze of prehistory, a dog protected the small group of hunter-gatherers that were your ancestors. Maybe, without dogs, you wouldn't be here.

How to Not Get into a Fight

———————————⟨∞⟩———————————

I grew up in rural Minnesota and went to a small high school — Eden Prairie High School, graduating class of 1968, a hundred students (GO EAGLES!) — where it was common, after high school football games, for teenage boys, with raging hormones and still-developing frontal lobes, to get into fights for no good reason. It was expected. Once during a game, a guy from Watertown, the opposing high school, came up to me and actually — with anger — said, "Do you want to fight?!" Not exactly subtle. I think he caught me looking at his girlfriend.

I made the mistake of laughing. (I wasn't a fighter.)

Next thing I knew I was on the ground with a bloody nose.

Eden Prairie honor besmirched, kids gathered around, then teachers. My assailant, outnumbered, decided it was time to split, and he left with his girlfriend — whom I recall looking back at me with interest, but maybe I was just concussed.

The moral of the story is, we could all learn from the signaling, negotiating, and fight-avoidance strategy of dogs.

For our purposes, I'm discussing normal, healthy dogs. That there are dogs bred to fight is repulsive, immoral, illegal, and any other word you want to add. Individuals who condone dogfighting as a sport should suffer the same fate as Ramsay Bolton in *Game of Thrones* (season six, episode nine: tied to a chair and killed by his own badly treated dogs).

Let me take a breath.

First, from an evolutionary point of view, fighting to kill or maim is a bad strategy unless it's unavoidable. In the wild, a wounded animal who wins a fight has a smaller chance of surviving, since they now have a higher probability of dying from infection or predation. Avoiding fights to the death or that cause serious injury makes evolutionary sense.

Wolves and dogs have evolved strategies to avoid conflict. In *Animals Make Us Human*, Temple Grandin notes that wolves have specific strategies for escalating or de-escalating conflict. Wolf puppies learn fifteen strategies (nine "dominance" strategies and six "submissive" strategies) to help them avoid actual blood-drawing fights. Interestingly, large "wolf-like" dogs like huskies and German shepherds tend to learn all fifteen strategies, while smaller dogs — like Maisie, our Chihuahua mix — tend to learn only a few of the strategies.

According to Grandin, examples of dominance behaviors are growling, teeth baring, "standing over" (one dog putting their head over the other's body), and standing erect (making themselves big). Submissive behaviors are muzzle licks, looking away, crouching, and passively submitting, that is, lying down and exposing their belly.

Among dogs, fights to the death are a rare occurrence; they occur mostly when dogs are cornered and afraid of being killed themselves. In the wild, one exception are fights over reproductive issues. (In my post–football game scuffle, sex was definitely an undercurrent.)

One of my heroes is the late psychiatrist Dr. Maxie Maultsby, who wrote that one of the essential skills for maturing is the ability to avoid or deescalate unnecessary conflict.

Among people, most day-to-day conflicts are unnecessary: "That parking space is mine!" "It was your turn to take out the garbage!" "The Red Sox suck!" "Those are my fries!"

In a dog's world, none of those things would cause conflict because, maybe wiser than us, they know how to deescalate.

We Live in a World of Sentience

The world is full of magical things,
patiently waiting for our senses to grow sharper.

— William Butler Yeats

I could never figure out what pigeons were *thinking*. I'd sit watching them for hours in the attic above the psychology department at Colorado College.

I could get them to turn left or right, or even a full circle, and to peck on a tray to get food pellets. It was a rote thing, done by thousands of undergraduates. Yet I had no idea what was going on in their heads. Although this inability seemed like a major flaw for someone interested in human psychology, I was instructed not to worry about it.

Because only behavior mattered.

The head of the department, the stern Dr. Roberts, sat underneath a picture of the father of behaviorism, the iconic and terrifying B.F. Skinner. There were two rules. First, humans were above and beyond every species in terms of intelligence no matter how it was measured. That was irrefutable. Don't talk about chimps and crows using tools. It was nondiscussable. Second, as far as animals were concerned there were no feelings, emotions, internal dialogue, moral quandaries, attachment issues, or the like. Even the idea that animals experienced pain was questioned. Animals possessed none of those messy "human" characteristics. There was just behavior that you could see and measure. My hard-science friends teased me that psychology was not really a science. In retrospect, I think that made many behaviorists defensive and reinforced their craving to *measure* something. My liberal arts brothers and sisters were aghast that we didn't consider the larger — and inner — lives of animals.

The prevailing wisdom, the greatest sin, the thing that would bring you wrath and red-pen critiques on papers was anthropomorphism. It was like a witch hunt or seeing Communists in every classroom — a popular pastime in the sixties.

Assigning human-like feeling or motivation to an animal (or gods) was the ultimate sign of unscientific thinking.

We were taught that we can't know if an animal is happy, sad, in pain, or angry. There was the standard essay question on psychology finals: "What animals feel pain?" Politically correct answer: not many.

To try to interpret behavior and assign emotions was a fool's errand.

That was the sea we swam in. That was the education I kowtowed to.

A note here about not questioning paradigms. In the sixties, using the prevailing understanding of dogs, the psychologist Martin Seligman was researching "learned helplessness."

Essentially, Seligman put dogs in a box where they

couldn't escape and gave them a mild shock. They'd jump up, but there was nothing they could do to avoid the shock. They were helpless. Later, when these same dogs were put in a box where they could escape the shock, they wouldn't even try. Learned helplessness became an important idea in psychology.

When I read about it, I never questioned the methodology. I just accepted the results and moved on. I was a product of the current scientific understanding: Dogs react to painful stimulus, but they can't "suffer."

Researcher Alexandra Horowitz, who wrote *Inside of a Dog: What Dogs See, Smell and Know*, teaches dog cognition at Barnard College. Unlike me, when she first read about Seligman's learned helplessness experiments, she was horrified. When I read her account, I felt terrible, not only because I didn't think of the suffering those dogs went through, but also because I had blithely accepted the dominate paradigm without thinking through the consequences myself. Now, I can't imagine putting any dog through an experiment like that, nor do I condone any animal research that deliberately causes pain.

This is another important dog lesson: *Question everything, especially if it results in the suffering of any being.*

Here is the rub. After a semester of behaviorism, I'd go home from school over the holidays and Rikka would be so glad to see me! I'd throw my backpack on the floor, and we'd roll around, play (another dangerously anthropomorphic word at that time), and chase each other down hallways until I was exhausted. She would sit, tongue hanging out of her mouth and a "grin" on her face.

It was confusing for an undergraduate: what I was being taught versus what I experienced in the world.

Today, thinking more deeply about anthropomorphizing, I feel, at its core, it is an arrogant idea: It is an anthropocentric approach to studying life and, for our purposes, dogs.

The idea is built on the presumption that human emotions are unmatched in the animal kingdom. Recent studies have debunked that line of thought.

To me, some of the most compelling are the fMRI studies of dogs done at Emory University in Atlanta. Dogs were trained to sit still, less than a millimeter of movement, in an fMRI machine. (I could never do that; score one for dogs.) Then they were subjected to a variety of stimuli, such as their human partner leaving and coming back into the room. Findings? Their dog brains responded in ways very similar to human brains when humans report feeling various specific emotions, like happiness.

In numerous other studies, scientists have measured levels of oxytocin in the blood of humans and dogs during petting sessions. Oxytocin is a hormone that facilitates bonding between humans, such as a mom and a nursing infant. Guess what? During those petting sessions, the oxytocin levels of both human and dog went up.

Other studies show that dogs, unlike any other animals, preferentially look at the right side of our faces. According to researchers, human emotions are more accurately represented on the right side of our faces. This might be a trait that dogs evolved over thousands of years to quickly ascertain the emotional state of us, their partners.

And just because I'm a romantic, think about whales for a moment. When I listen to the sounds of whales, the clicks and the pulsed and rhythmic calls, it is hard for me not to hear intelligence there. Their minds might be strange, foreign, nonhuman, and maybe unknowable, but they exist.

Charles Darwin (a dog lover) started us down the road of understanding where we came from and how we got here. Evolution is as powerful a theory as Galileo observing that the sun does not revolve around the earth. Now we are coming to grips with another philosophically earth-shattering idea: Our planet is full of sentience, or feeling and thinking life.

To quote the *Encyclopedia of Animal Behavior*: "Sentience means having the capacity to have feelings. This requires a level of awareness and cognitive ability. There is evidence for sophisticated cognitive concepts and for both positive and negative feelings in a wide range of nonhuman animals."

As for anthropomorphizing, I think we can all lighten up a bit. I'm coming from a formerly dogmatic point of view. Yet now I feel comfortable, because I know my dogs (like you know yours), to actually say out loud — Toby seems happy today, Maisie is afraid of thunder. I won't go as far as my four-year-old granddaughter, who said on one of our walks, "That tree is sad." I'm not there *yet*.

Then again, I try to remind myself, *question everything*.

Laurel Braitman, a Stanford-based science historian and expert in mental illness in animals, wrote, "It's not about anthropomorphizing, it's about anthropomorphizing well." For me, that will take some practice and unlearning. My goal is to understand the living world as it is and to deeply understand our dogs and appreciate them for who they are. For my granddaughter, my hope is that she will trust her intuition, distrust dogma, and investigate that sad tree idea.

The Importance of Touch

———— ⌒∽⌒ ————

Why do our current dogs (as all our family's dogs have done) jump up on our couch, put their heads on my lap, and just beg to be petted and held? Why do they lean against me? The reason is that touch is a fundamental — primal — need for most mammals (including humans). There have been numerous animal and human studies demonstrating that, when touch and physical contact are withdrawn, all sorts of bad health and psychological issues can arise. According to Nicole K. McNichols, human "infants literally cannot survive without human touch. Skin-to-skin contact even in the first hour after birth has been shown to help regulate newborns' temperature, heart rate, and breathing, and decreases crying."

Most healthy and bonded-to-you dogs seem to know this. They crave being petted, belly rubbed, to have a hand on their bodies.

It is a reminder, a teaching point (thank you, Toby), that we, too, need touch in our lives. Of course, between humans, especially strangers, getting consent, asking before touching, is important. Dogs don't bother with consent. Toby just barges into any situation, approaches any person on the street, and demands to be petted. That is fine with me. He is a wise dog.

A Dog's Reality

Reality is merely an illusion, albeit a very persistent one.

— ALBERT EINSTEIN

"Dad," I said enthusiastically, "did you know that there is no such thing as reality?" I was nineteen and had just finished my first college semester. He had picked me up at the airport for the Christmas holidays. As many new college students are, I was full of myself. The word *sophomoric* clearly defined me at that moment: a delusion of having superior intelligence.

My father paused, thought a moment, looked at me, and asked, "Have you been doing drugs?"

I stuttered and did not deny.

Then he put his hand on the board. "Car," he said. "Reality."

We were stuck in a long line of cars leaving the airport.

He motioned. "Traffic, reality."

Before I could clarify his clearly poor understanding of what I was trying to teach him, he added, "Your college tuition, reality."

I was apparently smart enough to remain silent.

Of course, he was right. After college (that wonderful

oasis surrounded by reality), there was work, money problems, relationships, marriage, kids, dogs, and the rapid
passing of time. All examples of reality.

And yet, putting my father's Minnesotan sensibilities
aside for a moment, when we dig a little deeper, reality —
yours, mine, and our dogs' — well, it gets interesting.

Let's start with the ancient parable of the blind men and
the elephant. Each man is asked to describe the elephant by
touching one part. One man touches the tusk, another the
legs, another the tail, and so on. Each then describes what
an elephant is using their limited information. In some tell-
ings of the story, the men come to blows over their conclusions, believing they are right, and the others have no idea
what they are talking about.

To widen our frame, imagine that the men are different
species, and they are trying to describe "reality." In this parable, let's say we ask a red-tailed hawk, a shrew, an octopus,
a mosquito, a whale, and a dog.

No doubt, each would provide profoundly different
descriptions, not only because their environmental niches
are so different, but because their *perceptions*, the ways they
sense their environment, are so different.

A daily example. We leave our house or apartment to
walk our dog. It's August. The park across the street is exploding in late summer blooms. Yet our dog can't see or appreciate the colors the way we do. A dog's normal vision has
red-green color blindness, so they can't distinguish between
those two colors.

Humans see more colors in the visible light spec-
trum, making us, by that measure, visually superior, but we

shouldn't get cocky. Like dogs, bees can't see red, either, but they can see ultraviolet light. And many flowers have an ultraviolet "target" that we can't see — as well as an electric charge bees can sense — which helps direct them to the nectar.

As we enter the park with our dog, we are looking, but our dogs are smelling. Molecules of all sorts are wafting through the air from the dirt, trees, plants, and hydrants and inundating our dog with smells. Dogs can see in dim light better than we can, but their perception of the world is largely driven by smell.

I have caught myself several times impatiently pulling my dog's leash when she stops to deeply smell a plant. I nudge her forward: *Gotta keep moving!* But that plant, which I mainly notice and sense visually, is an aromatic buffet for a dog. Imprinted in scent is a history of information: the rabbits that have grazed, the lizards that have scurried past, the other dogs that have peed. Yanking a dog away when they are smelling deeply is almost like putting a paper bag over someone's head in the middle of a dramatic movie so they can't see what happens next or how it ends.

Our experience of time is also a matter of perception. For instance, let's add a fly to our species-based "blind men and the elephant" parable.

Just like an old film movie, our brains receive a series of discrete images from our eyes that the brain then smooths out to create what we perceive as unbroken visual movement. Yet different species process different "frame rates." Humans see at a rate of about 60 images per second. Dogs are similar and see approximately 70 to 80 images per second. Yet the common house fly sees nearly 250 images a second, about four times faster than humans.

This means — here is the cool part — flies perceive time passing almost six times slower than humans. Thus, if a fly in the park lands on our arm, and we attempt to swat it away, the fly will see our arm move in what, to us, would be slow motion — easy for the fly to avoid.

The passage of time, which we measure with clocks, ticking or not, is not cast in stone. Every species perceives time differently. The question, of course, is who is right? As each species in our menagerie adds time to their descriptions of reality, even this won't be uniform, constant. So is everything relative? Is this what Einstein meant? Arrrgh!

I might add that our age also impacts our perception of time. At seventy, I find that time seems to gallop compared to those slow and boring hours in Mrs. Wanek's world history class when I was fifteen.

So if the point of our parable is that *the experience of reality is a function of perception*, then the real question is not whose perception is most accurate, but why have our senses evolved to be so different? The answer is that our senses work the way they do not to "grok" ultimate reality — evolution doesn't give a whit for our philosophical discourses on reality — but to help us survive as species in our own ways.

Welcome to *umwelt*.

The term *umwelt* was coined by Jakob Johann von Uexküll (1864–1944), a German biologist, and it roughly translates as "surrounding world or environment." My favorite definition of *umwelt* (which is cited in many places) is that "the mind and the world are inseparable because it is the mind that interprets the world for the organism."

Every organism has its own umwelt, its own perception of reality, built on its evolutionary past: the bee that buzzes by us, the fly we attempt to swat, ourselves admiring the colorful flowers, and our dog straining at the leash to inhale the scent of another dog's marking. This is true from the species swimming in the deep oceans to those running around our cities to parasitic wasps.

The other point of the parable — the true cautionary note — is that we are often so wedded to our perception of reality that we have difficulty letting go of it. Each man is certain that he understands the totality of what an elephant *is*, that he is experiencing all there is to experience. Our umwelt, almost by definition, is all-encompassing. This is why, in some versions of the story, the men fight over who is right. The idea that another person — or another species — might have a wholly different sense of the world can seem nonsensical, wrong, and a threat to us.

This brings us back to our companion dogs. They have their own rich umwelt. They perceive and respond to a world, a reality, that is different than humans.

I experience this almost daily while working at my desk. Toby will be sleeping at my feet. It's quiet, no sounds that I can hear except distant traffic. Suddenly, he jumps up and starts barking (and because he's Toby, howling). He is sensing — perceiving — a sound, a smell, a motion that I cannot. After a few minutes, he does a couple of circles around my feet and lies down again.

I have no idea what he is reacting to. In my reality, everything is fine. In his reality, danger is present.

So, as you walk your dog, take the time to notice what they notice. It's a different walk! Be careful not to fall into the trap of the blind men — thinking that what we perceive is all that there is, the "truth." It is not. Rather, be amazed at the complexity of cognition. As a dog buries their snout in a bush, and all life goes about its business, wonder at the many realities that exist.

It's Not Just about the Breed

Quick recap. Dogs and humans have long evolutionary histories. About forty thousand years ago, wolves and humans came together, began the process of "adopting and adapting," and over time wolves evolved into dogs that became, among other breeds, our present-day Chihuahua. A note: One Chihuahua recently sampled had a genetic link to the original (now-extinct) pre-Columbian North American dogs. Maisie, our Chihuahua mix, is extremely proud of that connection. However, I have avoided telling her that the Aztec's thought Chihuahuas were sacred. If she knew she descended from "royal" blood, we'd never hear the end of it. (She already sits on the back of our couch as if it were a throne.)

Next, although we share the same planet, neighborhoods, and homes, dogs and humans have different umwelts, different perceptions of the same environment. Not only can we not speak dog, but we also cannot *think* dog. We can infer how dogs perceive the world, but we can't know.

In full disclosure, frustrated by this lack of understanding, Laurie and I once contacted a dog psychic (via phone) to help us better understand our first Bernese mountain dog, Oso.

I know what you are thinking. Essentially, for fifty dollars, she told us that Oso *really* wanted to wear a red bandanna.

So, there's that.

The last piece of the puzzle, before we look at a philosophy of being with dogs, is to think about individual dogs, rather than types or breeds of dog. Remember, dogs have been with us for thousands and thousands of years. Official American Kennel Club (AKC) breeds have only existed since the late nineteenth century. For example, the Labrador was named an official breed in the early twentieth century.

Here is where it gets interesting, and for those who think that breeds determine behavior, maybe a bit controversial.

Laying down my cards, here is the mantra for this chapter: *It's not just the breed, it's the individual dog.*

Here is why I require a mantra.

I grew up with German shepherds. Our shepherds, Shawnee, Rikka, and later Max, were essentially guided missiles. Their MO was to go after (barking, growling, becoming fierce) anything or anybody that came to our home that was strange. We thought: *They're German shepherds. That is what they do.* Although our family rarely spoke of it, that was why we had them. Bunch of young kids, way out in the country with a dad who was gone a lot.

We did our best to warn people — delivery folks, my sisters' boyfriends. I'm convinced our dad was secretly thrilled. He was way too Catholic to talk to daughters about relationships (not that they would have ever listened), and he'd leave the room any time our more practical mom spoke to any of the girls about sex. Thus, two dedicated "mobile, hostile, agile" coconspirators suited him just fine.

We even had a sign in our driveway: "Don't get out of your car!!"

It was hand-painted by children on an old piece of plywood, with double exclamation marks to emphasize it was essential not to get out of the car.

It made perfect sense to us. But of course, to people new to us — new individuals, new delivery people, my sisters' newest boyfriends — they didn't know *why*.

We should've added, "DOGS! Stop your car in front of the door. Someone will come and escort you into the house...where you will be safe."

That would have focused any driver or errant lovestruck boy wandering or biking up our driveway.

Not only were our German shepherds "skeptical" about delivery people and boyfriends, they also had a thing about horses.

One of my father's money-making schemes was to board horses. The girls in the family had pleaded to get horses. Girls in my high school were constantly drawing pictures of horses. It was a farm/country thing. My dad and mom broke down, and our real, live cowboy grandfather Dinty went looking for saddle-broken horses. He ended up purchasing two. (He was once accused of painting a horse to sell it as an Appaloosa, but that's another story.) I put my foot down and told my dad I would not be involved in anything to do with the horses. He promised me that I wouldn't. Of course, within two months I was put in charge of morning feedings. Dinty imposed the "cowboy" way; that meant feeding the horses and dogs always came first before human breakfast. This meant up at 6 a.m. on school days, during the winter, because the girls and my kindergarten-aged brother needed more time to get ready for school. Making matters worse, to help defray the cost of having horses, our entrepreneurial father thought we could charge to board a couple more.

One July day, while I was mowing grass — a Sisyphean task in Minnesota in the summer — my sister Patty was walking the fence line with a bucket of oats. She was twelve. Peanuts, an American-bred stallion we were boarding, trotted up to the fence. Patty reached out to stroke his face, and the horse grabbed her arm in his teeth and began lifting her over the fence.

Before I could even shut the mower down, Shawnee's ears went to full alert. She sprang off the porch, sprinted the thirty yards to the fence, vaulted over the fence onto Peanuts's back, and bit down on his neck.

Peanuts let go of Patty, screamed in terror, and galloped off with Shawnee on her back. Shawnee jumped off, trotted back, slid under the fence, and lay down next to Patty, who was visibly upset. Fortunately, she was only bruised.

After that, Shawnee never let the horses next to any kids. Instead, she slid in between horse and kid and gently pushed the child away. We thought: *German shepherd*.

Most of the postal service drivers in our town knew us, and they stuck to the protocol. Drive up, honk horn, and wait until dogs quit biting their tires and someone connived the two shepherds with treats to come in the house. Then, and only then, was it safe to drop off packages.

But once, a new and innocent postal service driver drove up to our house. He apparently didn't take the driveway sign seriously. He got out of the truck and walked up to the door with a smile on his face. Before he could ring the doorbell or knock, my sister Patty opened the door, grabbed him by the lapels of his jacket, yanked him in, and slammed the door shut.

A second later, two German shepherds hit the door at full speed, chest high.

They had never barked....

He turned pale. As the dogs went crazy outside, Patty just shrugged it off and reminded the new driver to read the sign by the driveway. I recall that my mom invited him into the kitchen for a glass of water.

Thankfully, possibly because we were all so hypervigilant about the dogs, no one was ever bitten — maybe a couple of nips. (Our dog nip rules: If there was no blood, there was "no foul." If a bit of blood was drawn, put a Band-Aid on it and carry on. Most nipping happened during touch-football games or during pond-hockey games. Our dogs were competitive and played for the family teams.)

There were close calls. My sister Bonnie's boyfriend once drove up in a convertible with the top up. Sensing vulnerability, both dogs jumped on the car and began chewing through the canvas top.

Then one night it wasn't funny. It was autumn. I was fifteen. Our dad was out of town. The younger kids were getting ready for bed; Bonnie, who was thirteen, and I were doing homework. There was a knock at the door. The dogs began their synchronized barking. Automatically, my mom, Bonnie, and I went toward the front door, assuming it was one of Bonnie's friends.

Instead, there were two men, roughly dressed, standing

outside our door. It was cold. One of them appeared to be shivering. It was 1965, and I guess you could say we were naïve. One of the men said they were lost; they had tried to take a shortcut off the highway and ended up at our house. He asked if he could just use the phone.

Our mom looked at us, then at Shawnee and Rikka. They both had their ears up and were intently focused on the two men.

She nodded. Bonnie and I held the dogs. Our mom pointed to the phone in the living room. She gestured to us to sit with the dogs on the other side of the room.

One of the men took the phone, but his eyes were on the dogs. The other, who had been shivering, just sat there, still as could be, and stared. He sat still because any time he even flinched, both Shawnee and Rikka growled. Not a usual growl, but one that said this was a life-or-death situation for these guys, and they had better make the right decisions.

None of us spoke. I had never seen our dogs more alert and menacing.

There was a murmured phone call. Then, after the man hung up, he looked at his partner, whose eyes were wide open looking at our dogs.

He said, "Please hold on to your dogs. Our friend will pick us up on the road, now that he knows where we are. We're going to leave now."

As they slowly stood up, the hackles on the dogs went up. They growled again, deep and guttural.

The two men backed up toward the door, opened it, and disappeared into the night.

My mom grabbed the phone and called the sheriff. (There was no 911 then; the emergency numbers were taped to all our phones.) Two officers drove by, searched around our house, and found no one. Mom gave them a description. They left, and that was that.

I've always wondered why our mom let them in the house. In retrospect, I think she felt sorry for the one who was shivering. I also think, in a Machiavellian way, that instead of letting them snoop around the house and sneak in, she wanted them to meet the dogs that would give their lives to protect us.

They were our defenders. At night, you'd hear them patrolling the house. They rarely left our sight. They were "being" exactly how we wanted them to be. Mostly. During touch-football games, it was annoying when they'd run away with the ball.

Given all this you can understand that we assumed that our dogs were genetically predisposed that way.

They're German shepherds.

That presumption does leave out some critical information. Neither of them was "socialized." What does that really mean? It was a fair question in rural Minnesota back then. We didn't have dog parks. Puppy play dates? Taking German shepherd puppies to a mall to just meet people? We lived in a "no dogs allowed" culture.

Had we done all those things, especially when they were puppies, our two guided missiles would've been much different dogs, maybe less guided missile and more inquisitive and fun-loving.

Here is where the current research stands. As much as we stereotype breeds, a dog's breed is not a good predictor of the *behavior* of an individual dog. Whereas physical traits are good predictors of a dog's breed, one study found that "breed offers little predictive value for individuals, explaining just 9 percent of variation in behavior."

The study said one behavioral trait called "biddability" — that is, how well a dog does our "bidding," or responds to human direction — was the most heritable by breed, but it still varied significantly among individual dogs in a breed category.

For example, our German shepherds, as predicted, were usually good at playing "get the stick" or even coming when called. Our current Great Pyrenees, Toby, not so much. He does what he wants when he wants. The idea of doing our bidding is probably insulting to him.

In sum, this goes to show how complicated and intriguing the "nature-nurture" discussion has become.

All dogs come from ancestral dogs that coevolved with us to be friendly and to (probably) guard, hunt, or herd. There is no such thing as a "blank slate" dog. Modern-day human-directed breeding (done over a tiny amount of time compared to the thousands of years of evolution) has focused primarily on the physical aspects of dogs, from huskies to spaniels. An exception is individuals who breed dogs to be aggressive fighting dogs or passive "bait" dogs. You know what I think about those individuals.

Inside each breed there is as much behavioral variation as that found between breeds. This explains why some of our later German shepherds were laid-back compared to our Chihuahua mix, Maisie, who thinks she's a rottweiler (a rottweiler *trained* to be a guard dog).

This has significant implications for someone looking to adopt a dog. If you are looking for certain kinds of behavior from a dog, don't just consider the breed. Rather, get to know the individual dog, and maybe their parents, and (HUGE) how they were treated in the first three months of life.

And like me, just keep repeating the mantra: *It's not just the breed, it's the individual dog.*

The Importance of Naps

Most dogs' default activity, when they are done running, eating, barking, or doing whatever they do, is to nap. I have always been impressed with this quality. All our dogs have had the ability to be going at Mach 5, then just stop, curl up, and fall asleep. Most dogs sleep more than twelve hours a day, with puppies sleeping up to eighteen hours and old dogs often sleeping just as much.

It's the ability to just fall asleep anywhere, anytime, that impresses me. Dogs are polyphasic, meaning they often take naps multiple times during the day. Humans, probably for cultural reasons more than anything else, are monophasic, sleeping only at night. Although, ask any parent of young kids — or any medical resident, firefighter, cop, or soldier — and they will tell you that the ability to fall asleep, like a dog, when the right moment arises, no matter what time of day or night, is crucial to maintaining awakeness when needed and thus sanity. Many people worry about napping. They feel guilty, as if they should be doing something. I say, when the moment offers itself, NAP! Take a lesson from your dog. You'll wake up refreshed and ready to chase balls, do work, or whatever makes your day.

LOVING-KINDNESS

May all beings be happy and secure,
may they be happy-minded.

— METTA SUTTA, TRANSLATED BY PETER HARVEY

The Buddhist loving-kindness meditation above begs the question, how do we choose to interact with our first non-human partners?

A story to start.

Laurie and I once adopted a puppy, a totally black German shepherd. She came to us in the back of a pickup truck filled with her brothers and sisters.

It was dark night — an important detail. The human "mom" driving the truck told us that she was the runt of the litter, and all the other puppies had been spoken for. Laurie gathered her up in her arms and took her in the house, while I signed papers and wrote a check.

The pickup truck rattled down the road, and I went in to meet our newest dog. She was clearly not an energetic puppy. She was comfortably resting in Laurie's arms and showed no interest in exploring her new home.

After a few minutes, I thought it would be a good idea to take her outside to pee. I picked her up, went out the front door, put her down, and she immediately bolted into the trees. I could not see her. I called to Laurie to get a flashlight, and I started to run in the direction she had taken (probably scaring her to death).

My heart was in my throat.

It took a long ten minutes before I finally found her. She had wandered back to the house. Whether on purpose or by mistake, we had no idea. We brought her into the house and decided to name her Sombra, Spanish for shadow. She had disappeared into the night shadows, and we thought that we might have lost her.

Those few minutes gave me the visceral understanding of our relationship with dogs. She was young, vulnerable, and would not survive without human aid.

Thinking about that night, I have come to a couple of conclusions.

First, the language that we use about the dog-human relationship is not helpful. The idea of "owning" a dog doesn't fit how I feel. I've "owned" cars. I've watched two of them burn to the ground (unrelated, long stories). I had no real emotional attachment them.

Further, "owning a dog," which has been the prevailing paradigm for generations, leads to all sorts of abuse: from chaining dogs to training them to fight, to neglecting them, and to disposing of them when they become old or "useless" or don't fit into a lifestyle anymore.

Here is your essay question: *Can you "own" a sentient being?*

Words are important; they shape how we think. How we think governs how we act.

Even though there is often money exchanged, we don't "buy" a dog. It's much closer, and makes more philosophical sense, to think that we are "adopting" a dog. For instance, money is often exchanged when adopting a child — there are adoption fees — but we never say we're "buying" a baby.

I prefer to replace the concept of "owning" and the title of "owner" with the term *guardian*.

I love the idea of being a guardian — a defender, protector, keeper — for our dogs. Dogs need guardians. They are smart, and also often idiots. They are much like the teenage boys I coach on the soccer pitch. If not on leashes, they will chase cars — the dogs, not the teenagers — although if bored enough, the boys might be up for a chase.

My job as a guardian is to keep our dogs safe.

Another job as a guardian is to assure that our dogs are growing and happy. A baseline for having a dog is allowing a dog to be part of the family, with freedom to roam in a house (when they are house-trained) and to have frequent walks or runs.

Another distinction: Objects that I "own" serve me, but as a dog guardian, I try to make sure our dogs are allowed to satisfy and be themselves. Dogs get the zoomies, they mark with urine, and they bark...sometimes a lot. (Toby, are you listening? Nope, he's howling at that *Modern Family* theme music.) If dogs are not harming anyone or another dog, we can relax and just let them be dogs.

Dogs also need our care and attention, and that is where loving-kindness as a philosophy can help us frame the relationship. As a dog guardian, you probably already feel this as you watch your dog take that morning nap in the sun.

Loving-kindness is the first "heart practice" of Buddhism.

In Buddhism it's called *metta*. Practicing metta is a two-step process. First, meditate on loving-kindness and what that means to you. I try to be conscious about how I want to be in the world. I'm not perfect at it, yet there are times — standing in a long line, feeling myself getting hooked into an argument, being cut off in traffic — when I focus on the idea of being kind. It helps! It also helps lower my stress.

Second, put metta into practice daily with actions: kindness, friendliness, openheartedness.

For me — sometimes this is easy, other days a challenge — I intentionally look for opportunities to be kind. This can be simple things like opening doors or letting drivers move in front of me in traffic. I find the benefit of simple acts of kindness is that they make me feel better.

As you probably have guessed, I use this same philosophy with dogs and all living, sentient creatures.

A weird little story about mice to illustrate.

When Laurie and I built a house outside of Santa Fe, one of the construction folks told me that during the excavation he noticed mice everywhere. He quipped there was "an explosion of those critters" every time they moved brush from the housing site. It's the high desert and it was a wet summer. Mice had proliferated. I didn't think much about it until we moved in.

Of course, the mice loved our house and also moved in. Not good. They are pests, they have litters seemingly every week, and we began finding their poop everywhere. Baby mice began falling out of the ceiling of our living room. And bonus! In New Mexico, we were beginning to see the first cases of hantavirus, a serious and often fatal respiratory disease that is spread by mice feces. (Fun fact: New Mexico is also home to the rodent-driven bubonic plague.)

In our house, we have distinct screams. There is the "snake in the house" scream and the distinct "mouse ran over my feet" scream. Infamously, there is also the "pack rat jumped off the wall onto my head" scream — that was me.

As the "mouse in the house" screams became more frequent, the edict came down from on high (Laurie and our daughters) that it was up to me to make our house mouse-free. Initially, our daughters wanted me to livetrap the mice and take them to a field by our house and set them free! That did not pan out.

So I set traps. I trapped a lot of mice. I also "trapped" my finger a couple times whilst loading the standard mouse traps. That loud *snap* sound still haunts my dreams. I'd put the dead mice outside by the driveway and the crows would take them: circle of life.

Then, one day when I was in a hardware store buying more traps, the customer-service guy suggested I try glue traps: No more fingers caught, and they are more efficient at trapping mice.

I bought a few, tried them, and was horrified. Most often the trapped mice were not killed; they were just caught in the glue and slowly died from suffocation or exhaustion. When my kids saw this, they were upset and angry — at me, of course. As a note, a dorm at Harvard a few years back revolted when they discovered the custodians were using glue traps. They were divinity students, no doubt closer to the spiritual than I.

Here's the gist: We had to rid our house of mice *and* we had to do it humanely.

To some eyes, this may seem foolish, but not to preteen daughters. And the truth is, we kill all sorts of animals all the time, especially for food. In my view, this is necessary and not "evil." Temple Grandin, the animal behaviorist, wrote, "I think using animals for food is an ethical thing to do, but we've got to do it right. We've got to give those animals a decent life and we've got to give them a painless death. We owe the animal respect."

Giving an animal a painless death. That was all I was after, even for mice.

So, I gingerly went back to the traditional traps and later tried battery-powered electric-shock traps. They kill the mice instantly, no suffering. The kids were happier (they still occasionally lobbied for the "set them free" approach), and I had a lighter conscience.

If you think this story opens a can of worms, you're right. Once we accept the idea that the world is full of sentience, and that loving-kindness is the approach we want to embody, this is a dilemma we face daily.

No one said this was easy.

We have a choice to make: We can live conscious of the dilemma that as humans we have an inordinate impact on the living world, both directly and indirectly, or we can choose to move through our lives oblivious. The problem is that once we become aware of the life around us, and of the harm we do even unintentionally, it is hard to unsee it. Thus we all need to make choices, to draw our lines about what is acceptable and what is not, about what is ethical and what is not. Daily I make decisions. Cut down on meat? Drive in a cautious way not to hit an animal? (I killed a deer once when I was a teenager; it was a nightmare.) Be aware of insecticides and other poisons that creep up the food chain? Move a spider in the sink outdoors? Everyone's "line" is different. A tenet of the Indian Jainist religion is that you may not harm any living being — it's the highest ethical tradition of that sect. For others, the line might be eating less meat, or not eating certain animals, or not eating any animals. The point is to live our lives consciously aware of the impact we have and to think about how to "lighten" our footprint.

Dogs are my touchstone. They daily pull me out of my anthropocentric mindset and remind me of the nature of the world we live in, full of life, different intelligences, all clinging to the same planet. We are stewards of that planet now; whole ecosystems depend on our decisions. A bit of loving-kindness helps us all.

What Happened to the Wallpaper?

"Loving-kindness" is our family's philosophy of how we want to treat our dogs. Admittedly, that leads to some relaxed attitudes about daily life with dogs. Leashes when we walk only because it's the law. Free-roaming dogs in the wilderness. Dogs on the furniture; the beds, the couches, the chairs. Dogs in the kitchen while we cook. No real sense of any human as the alpha.

Our dogs have the run of the house and act as if they own the place.

Not surprisingly, this was also how Laurie and I raised our kids. And no, as the dad, I was not the alpha with them, either. I'm not sure any father of teenage daughters ever is. Our pecking order, after our kids became teens, was Laurie, the girls, and then whatever female dog we lived with. Any male dog and I vied for second-to-last place.

Of course, the philosophy of loving-kindness had some unintended consequences.

At first, I thought we had been robbed. We'd been gone for ten days, and we had left the dogs with a trusted dog sitter, Jill. Since she worked nine-to-five, her plan was to walk them in the morning, be gone all day, and then take care of them at night.

As we carried our bags into the kitchen, Laurie noticed a note on the table that simply read, "Sorry! Call me!"

The dogs surrounded us as we came in. They were joyous, barking and jumping up on us. But we could tell something else was going on with them. A whiff of guilt? A touch of remorse? A little too much enthusiasm? (Yes, I'm anthropomorphizing!)

We lugged our suitcases into the living room and stopped cold.

Open-mouthed, we both looked at what was left. The first couch we ever bought, shredded. Books on the floor. Pillows ripped apart. It looked like someone had not only robbed us, they had been deliberately searching for valuables hidden in the couch and the bookshelves. I had a cousin who had just been paroled after committing grand larceny, so that is where my mind immediately went.

Still speechless, Laurie pointed to the wall, where strips of wallpaper hung down. What robber would do that?

As we stood there in shock, Zuni, a one-year-old shepherd and the newest member of our clan, stood loyally by my side, leaning into me as if he, too, was shocked, just shocked!

The other two dogs, maybe wiser and older, had already asked to be let outside, perhaps to get as far away from any retribution as possible once we figured out what had happened.

Laurie called Jill, who was all of nineteen. Breathlessly, she explained — while apologizing every five seconds — that she had come home from work and found the living room destroyed. She, too, had thought, *Crime!*...until she saw Zuni with a pillow in his mouth.

Busted.

I looked at Zuni, and he looked back at me with those deep brown eyes as if to say, *What?*

I thought if Zuni was the culprit — and I wasn't letting our other two dogs off the hook just yet — it was so uncharacteristic. He was a shy dog. When we had people over, he'd retreat to the farthest bathroom and sit behind a toilet. When I was working, he'd curl up under my desk.

Had this happened when I was growing up, my dad would've taken Zuni by the collar, put his snout in the pillow, and firmly said, "No!" He would've called a family meeting, to be greeted with downcast eyes. No one would have admitted that we probably had been using pillows to play fetch with the dogs, and the floor was lava and we had to jump from couch to couch.

As Zuni gazed at me, I understood he had no memory of doing anything wrong. Putting his snout in the pillow and saying no would just confuse him.

As you can see, our hippie-like style of guardianship — all the folderol of letting dogs be dogs — was occasionally an expensive choice.

That said, if teenagers were left in a house, unable to leave and with no supervision for hours, well, good luck! They'd burn down the house as a science experiment.

Dogs get bored. They get lonely. They miss their humans. They act out.

What we were learning, slowly, day by day, was that our philosophy of dog — kind, loving, and forgiving — takes work. It takes a little bit of sacrifice, as well as time, energy, and attention, to raise happy dogs.

It's a daily thing. They need exercise, playtime, and time to have their bellies rubbed. Most importantly, because they are social animals, they need to be with us. Devoted time and actions bring this philosophy to life.

Here is the elephant-in-the-room question: If it takes time, effort, and "being" with dogs to raise happy dogs, then in our time-crunched existences, can anyone and everyone be a dog guardian?

Of course, the answer is no.

When I was in college, I made the mistake of thinking I could have a dog. I lived with six other students in a big house in Colorado Springs. On impulse one day, I drove to Pueblo, Colorado, adopted a German shepherd puppy, and named him Alyosha. (I was a pretentious Russian literature major at the time. Don't ask.) I thought I knew everything I needed to know about "having" a dog.

It was a disaster.

I couldn't take him with me to classes. I had to study a lot (a slow student, was I). My roommates were less than enthusiastic about a dog in the house. Keeping him in my room and then walking with him once or twice a day was an unfair life, no matter how much I cared for him.

I decided the best thing to do was bring him home and invite him to join the Minnesota clan. Before I could make arrangements, somehow, someway, Alyosha escaped from our house and ran away. I put up signs, visited the shelter, but to no avail. He was lost. I was crushed. I had made the cardinal mistake of thinking that having a dog was "cool" rather than understanding that having a dog is a relationship.

Relationships = time, focus, and daily work.

After that, I chose not to have a dog until I understood more, until I had the time and, importantly, a partner who could help.

Back in our living room, we cleaned up the mess while the dogs lounged (looking a little guilty?) and watched. We put the books back and rescued a couple of pillows. The couch was a total loss (our dog ate our couch!), and the wallpaper would have to wait for another day.

That night, as our dogs settled in, I thought of Alyosha and what had happened to our house. They were related. The practical lesson is that we can't leave dogs by themselves for long periods of time. Trainers have mixed opinions on how long is too long. With our current escape artist, Toby, four hours alone is about all he can manage before he tries to escape. This has had far-reaching consequences for how we schedule work, vacations, business trips, and when we needed to call in a dog sitter.

The larger lesson goes back to understanding dogs and us as species. No matter how much "individualism" is idolized, no matter how much blather we are inculcated with about "the Lone Ranger," "Pull yourself up by your own bootstraps," it is evolutionary nonsense. We — dogs and humans — are social animals, meant to be in tribes, packs, clans, and family. We drift away from those roots at our peril. We have an epidemic of loneliness, of being adrift without a purpose. Our postindustrial age conflicts with our deep evolutionary roots.

When that culturally induced "individuality" construct starts pulling at me, I close my eyes and imagine an Amish barn-raising. A community coming together to work and be together. It calms me down and helps me remember that I am one of many, and we evolved to be together...with our dogs.

Loving-kindness. Energy, time, together.

Part 3

Living in Wild Country

*Nature might have made Sphinxes in her spare time or
Mona Lisas with her left hand, blindfolded. Instead,
she gave us the grain of sand, the polished river stone,
the Grand Canyon....After the Artist, only the copyist.*

— Jerry and Renny Russell, *On the Loose*

Laurie and I were in our thirties. We had jobs. We'd moved from the city, where Riva was constantly escaping, to a more dog-friendly location in the farmlands of Minnesota. Yes — he writes a bit defensively — we moved because of dogs, just like parents move to be in better school districts. Our new home was an old honey farm that was built in 1921. (Another magical place that would be plowed under for mini-mansions. Do people look at a beautiful barn and think, "Yep, we can tear that down and put in a five-car garage"?)

Our dog-centric family had grown: We had no kids yet, but we had Nugie, our collie, and Riva, and we'd added Zuni, his New Mexico name foreshadowing a big move coming up.

I was pretty much a Minnesota boy. I loved winters (weird, I know), and I loved where we lived. I had a good job and a stable income. And the dogs were perfectly content with a big yard and lots of open spaces.

I could see us living there forever.

So obviously, it was time to move.

There are all sorts of romantic reasons people move to Santa Fe. Individuals pack up their car and run from bad relationships, bad bosses, crowded cities, and pandemics. They sell their Toyota Camry and buy a used Ford 150 pickup, hoping to reinvent themselves in New Mexico — Santa Fe being a serious contender for the "reinvention" capital of the USA. In the 1990s musical *Rent*, the protagonist sings about leaving New York and opening a restaurant in Santa Fe (not Eden Prairie, Minnesota). Some want to become cowgirls or cowboys (hard work!). Others are drawn because

New Mexico has a reputation for being a spiritual place. Spiritual, I surmise, because of all the Tibetan prayer flags flying in Santa Fe and Taos, and the roadside *descansos*, or memorials, everywhere.

Then there are those who intend to just pass through on their way to LA, realize this is the most beautiful place they've ever seen, and never leave. It's because of the sky, the horizons, the aspens on the face of the mountains that glimmer a hallucinogenic green in the rain. Santa Fe being Santa Fe, in the eighties there were a lot of bumper stickers that read "Welcome to Santa Fe...now go home!" To have that bumper sticker, your family needed to have lived there for at least five generations.

Anyway, we came for a more prosaic reason: Laurie got a job.

THE ROAD TO SANTA FE

If you drive west all night from Minnesota, as the sun rises behind you, you will find yourself near Julesburg, Colorado, along the South Platte River. In front of you, *in the soon to be future*, the Rockies appear. Although the night is still pitch black, the morning sun glints off the snowy peaks. The prairies — those of the Indigenous tribes and the buffalo — rise, rise from Julesburg to the foothills of the Rockies and the mysteries beyond. "Eastward I go only by force; but westward I go free," Thoreau wrote.

Driving on Interstate 80, I could feel the pull.

I had gone to a little college in Colorado, had driven this route multiple times, and now here I came again. This time with Laurie and three sleepy dogs in the back toward a new home.

If you believe that geography is destiny, it is never clearer than driving west. Cities, malls, congestion, and traffic melt away to open horizons. In the nineteenth century, when it was all still new and mysterious, romantics of the West wrote about leaving not only crowded cities but the rigid caste systems of the East for possibilities, new ideas, and Jeffersonian ideals.

Iowa, Nebraska, eastern Colorado went by as a blur at eighty miles an hour. Sitting in the car while Laurie drove, I closed my eyes and imagined wagon trains full of idealists and seekers moving at twenty miles a day (on a good day) following the Platte. Now, that same distance took us fifteen minutes.

Today, unlike in 1821, during the days of the Santa Fe Trail, if you want to keep openness in front of you, you need to make a screeching left-hand turn south on I-25 before the Denver megalopolis brings your westward progress to a crawl and swallows you up.

South we went, down past the Front Range boom towns, across the border to New Mexico — a place that hundreds of thousands of Americans (who didn't have Sister Mildred to teach them the US states in fifth grade) still believe is part of Mexico.

Six hours later, we pulled into the sleepy, weird, and different town of La Villa Real de la Santa Fe de San Francisco de Asís, also known as Santa Fe.

And so the adventure began.

"Don't stop!" Laurie yelled, "or we'll be stuck for good!" She was hanging on to the dashboard as the truck leaned hard left.

Santa Fe mud is special. It's caliche mud, slick as wet ice, and once you're stuck in it, it's like cement. Based on advice from native Santa Feans, we had left our "city" car in town and borrowed a Suburban to drive to our rental house. With three dogs in the back, the goal was to stay in the center of the road. But like a drunk trying to walk a straight line, the truck kept leaning and slipping to the left. Although we were leaning hard to the right, we ended up in the ditch.

Wap! Wap! Wap! The sideview mirror hit every wooden

fence post as I accelerated and tried my best to get us back on the road. The dogs barking at cattle did not help.

After a few "exhilarating" moments, we made it back onto the old ranch road and reached the house. I turned off the engine and rested my head on the steering wheel. The sideview mirror was hanging by a couple of wires.

The white truck was now totally mud covered, a rich dark brown. Turns out, in winter, most cars and trucks in Santa Fe are the same color. With lots of dirt roads, there's a certain cachet about having a car (and boots and jeans) covered in mud. *Yippee ay yay!*

We opened the doors and the dogs leaped out. The house had one neighbor half a mile away. The road was impassable. There were vistas as far as the eye could see, with the mountains in the distance. The sky was so brightly blue that it was hard to look at.

Heaven.

The three of them, Riva, Nugie, and Zuni, started exploring this new place. Roving in concentric circles, they were smelling new things — mostly dirt, with a touch of snow, piñons, and juniper. Not a lot else. Dinty, my cowboy grandfather, passed by Santa Fe ranch country a few months later and remarked that even jackrabbits would have to pack a lunch to survive here. (He also said he only bought blue jeans that when new could stand up by themselves. A cowboy thing.)

The dogs kept looking back at us: *Where's the fence? How far can we go?* Realizing that the answer was no limits, they were off like a shot. Here was a test of loyalty. Would they keep going — maybe head home to the gentle hills of Minnesota — or circle back?

As we unpacked the Suburban, I watched them out of the corner of my eye.

There is no place like Santa Fe to remind you of deep history. The First People trekked along the shores of ancient Lake Otero, now White Sands National Park, possibly twenty-three thousand years ago. They were followed by multiple cultures: the Anasazi, the Pueblo people, the Apache raiders, the Navajo to the north, the Spanish, then the Americans. There have been wars and millennia-long, civilization-ending droughts.

The geology is naked before you: deeply carved arroyos, the basalt remnants of ancient volcanoes. In the distance is the Valles Caldera, a volcano that exploded a million years ago, expelling shards of obsidian, a glass-like mineral that the Native Americans used to make arrowheads and which is still used in surgeries today.

The town backs up to national forests that carpet the mountains in every direction. Coming from the green and rolling hills of the north, I found it a wondrous landscape.

It was all new. I felt as if passports should be required to come to Santa Fe. There were signs about not bringing guns into movie theaters. In 2022, because of permissive gun laws, those signs are reappearing. There were roads with no names. On our first drive into town, I couldn't help but notice loose dogs everywhere. There were streets "downtown" so narrow that two cars could barely pass each other. You had to get used to the mud-brown architecture. Awesome "low-rider" cars paraded around town on Saturday nights.

Schools were let out early on Fridays so kids could go skiing. There were drive-through liquor stores. Coming from Minnesota (land of on-time rule followers), I felt people had lax feelings about laws in general: Stop signs were a suggestion. Yellow traffic lights meant go. Drinking and driving: a slap-on-the-wrist offense. Laurie was rear-ended by a drunk driver within six months of living there. He sped off and crashed into a liquor store: karma.

Like tourists everywhere — and we are all basically tourists, if you think about it — we knew nothing about this place. We had yet to understand that we now lived in a wilder place than Minneapolis. We had yet to contend with coyotes, bears, mountain lions, black widows, rattlesnakes, and those loosely connected dogs.

Laurie worked at a conference center that was an old ranch on the Pecos River forty miles from Santa Fe. Technically, the ranch was ceded to the local communities by the 1848 Treaty of Guadalupe Hidalgo. But no matter, in the nineteenth century, Anglos "bought" the land and kept it — a kind of "finders keepers" colonialist thing.

One of the locals told Laurie that occasionally packs of dogs roamed through the property. The best thing to do in those situations was to stay indoors until they left.

As we moved into our new temporary home, this was all in front of us.

Fortunately, that first day, our dogs chose loyalty over total freedom. They came back together, nipping at each other, trotting, and went into the house with no begging from me. They slurped up water that Laurie had put out in bowls and then collapsed on the floor.

A good sign.

In the early days, I felt that if I died and was buried here, the earth would spit me out because I was a stranger. The landscape, so big, so different, was disorienting. I'd run with the dogs. We'd get lost in the arroyos and need to climb to a high point so that we could find ourselves. The dogs, always adaptable, quickly learned that the summer was about finding shade, and in the winter, shafts of sunlight. They learned about the howls of coyotes, and this new creature, the jackrabbit.

Here is the deal: Once you've seen a truly blue sky, once you've experienced a two-foot snowfall, a mountain blizzard, followed immediately by blue skies and 50-degree temperatures, once you've seen a horizon one hundred miles away, it works on your soul. You want to kick yourself for not knowing that this place existed.

Thus, a year later, we bought a house in the last hills of the southern Rocky Mountains. The two of us and three dogs. We were next to the national forest. From our house we could walk the ridgelines all the way to Colorado and never see a soul.

As former suburban folk, we moved in without thinking about what it meant to live in the New Mexican wilderness. You give up a lot. True to our Santa Fe friend's warning, the three-mile dirt road to our house destroyed the suspensions of our "city" cars. There was no internet, barely phone service, and when it snowed, we were stuck.

What we received in turn was the sound of wind through trees. Coyotes howling day and night. Sun rising on the mountains. Two minutes from our house we could drop down into an arroyo and go back five hundred years. Finding Pueblo pottery shards in the arroyo washouts was common. And darkness! Have you ever stood outside and experienced true darkness? On moonless nights it was so dark we couldn't see ten feet.

Riva and I would stand under starlight, a human and dog. As I heard her breathing, I had that ancient desire to know what she was thinking. What did she think as she smelled the Rocky Mountain night? How could she not be changed? Riva had lived with us in city apartments, a tiny city house, and a suburban farm. She had chased me through the deep snowdrifts of a Minnesota blizzard, ran with me down country roads. Now we were standing on the edge of the universe: the Milky Way above and the ancient Rockies laid out at our feet.

Geography is destiny.

Later in our dog world, Toby, the Great Pyrenees, who was born out West, would hear coyotes howl, and he'd just bark in warning. For Riva, the howling of a wild "dog-adjacent" being was brand new. Her ears perked up, her head slanting to the side as if to hear better. Did she think of the calls as a threat? Or did she think they were calling to her? On those special nights, just Riva and me, the cacophony of howls, yips, cries, and short barks surrounded us. Did the wild voices stir in her a primordial lust to join them? To go back in time?

Unknowable.

It wasn't a foreign thought. I had been told the story of a Maine Outward Bound instructor. One day, because he was free and unfettered, he stood on a road close to the national forest. He stripped off all his clothes and strode into the wilderness. There he built a shelter, made clothes, and fed himself. Months later, he stepped back onto the road, having proved that he could survive (thrive?) in the woods. He stood on the road, watched traffic zoom by, and he turned back and chose wilderness.

Of course, neither I nor Riva was free and unfettered. We were tied to home, family, and all the pulls of American adulthood. Thoreau wrote, "If you are ready to leave father and mother, and brother and sister, and wife and child and friends, and never see them again, if you have paid your debts, and made your will, and settled all your affairs, and are a free man, then you are ready for a walk."

Riva and I were not quite there. We'd made other choices.

Yet we stood there together, leaning against each other, me with my hand on her rough German shepherd fur. Was this what it was like in the beginning of human, dog, and wilderness? Unspoken, together gazing out on a wild world? I think so. And even though we both loved sleeping inside and having food and water at the ready, in those moments there was a connection to something larger than us, to the earth, the forests, the mountain lakes, and winter snow: *to Oneness.*

I was thinking: *someday.* She'd look up at me with that brown-eyed steady gaze, and I'm almost certain she was thinking the same thing: *someday.*

In the Wilderness

It was our first October in our new home. One night we were watching one of the three fuzzy TV channels we could receive with our rabbit-ear antennas.

Suddenly, Zuni and Riva started an enormous racket and began clawing at the kitchen door. (Nugie, the collie, also barked but did it from a couch.)

I opened the door and they burst out. They both got about ten yards, hit the brakes at the same time, turned around, and sprinted back in the house and into the back bedroom. As I peered out, a hulking shape with our plastic garbage can in its mouth was casually walking down the driveway. A black bear.

In Minnesota, our dogs had dealt with chipmunks, squirrels, deer, and raccoons. There was also the occasional skunk (white vinegar, baking soda, and dish soap, mixed, will take care of that). But nothing in their lives had prepared them, or me, for a bear.

There were also coyotes. They seem ubiquitous now, but when we moved West, it was the first time I had heard or seen them.

Zuni, Riva, and I were running a trail (Nugie: not a runner). We had gone about a mile when we turned down an arroyo and smack into a pack of coyotes. We had been downwind of them, so they were as surprised as we were.

The dogs' hackles went up and they started barking. I also started barking. The coyotes scattered (this time…), but it was a reminder that we were not in Kansas, um Minnesota, anymore.

As for snakes, I had basically grown up in the bottoms of the Minnesota River, so I was familiar with big bull snakes. One late night I dove into a pool right on top of a six-foot bull snake. I aged years.

New Mexico has rattlers. The problem with our dogs was that they were oblivious to snakes. Snakes were not something on their list of stuff they needed to warn us about. A rabbit in the garden caused an insane amount of barking, but a potentially deadly snake? Oblivious.

In our second summer, a snake (unidentified) got into the house. It apparently slithered past a sleeping Riva and found a hole in the wallboard and disappeared. Laurie watched, did her "snake scream," and yelled my name. We had a snake stuck between the wallboard and the frame of the house. From there, it could go anywhere. I explained this to Laurie, and in so many words she said it was unacceptable. I called a friend, Pete (safety in numbers), and we did what any two snake-aware guys who were not contractors would do: We tore out the wall where the snake was. Nothing.

The snake had disappeared.

During all the commotion and Laurie's realization that we might have a permanent new resident, the dogs were blasé. They were unmoved that their humans were upset, failing to realize we wanted them to at least show some interest.

As we debated what to do, Laurie leaned against the banister that led to the upstairs office.

She was facing me. Behind her, wrapped around the banister, was our guest, less than a foot away. I whispered to Laurie, "Don't move."

Naturally, she took that as a signal to move. She turned around, saw, yelled, and jumped back. Then the dogs (finally) sprang into action. By that I mean they barked in unison.

Pete and I quickly recognized that the snake wasn't a rattler; it was just a big bull snake. I unraveled it from the banister and took it outside and let it go with an admonition to not come back.

For all of us, this was another lesson in the class we were taking, New Mexico wilderness 101. And like us, the dogs still had a lot to learn about living in the high desert and the mountains. For example, all three dogs had to have cactus encounters before they learned to watch where they were going.

My biggest anxiety for all three dogs was living without a fenced yard. I was afraid they'd take off and get lost or chase the rare car and get hurt. Loose dogs lived three miles down our road. They continually chased our cars; it was a daily contest to outwit them and not hit them.

I needn't have worried about our guys. They stuck close to home, and as a result they had the best of all possible dog worlds: freedom to roam, no leashes, a home, and their humans to be with.

I learned to trust them. It turned out that they were all "homebodies" like we were. Later we would have dogs we couldn't trust to be off-leash for a minute.

We settled into a routine. After checking for bears and snakes, we'd hike and go on runs. Laurie would come home from work and be greeted by three enthusiastic dogs. I worked at home. I was a prepandemic experimenter in remote work. I was connected to our office via modem at the then-shockingly fast speed of 300 baud. Write all morning. Send document while having lunch — it took an hour to send. Repeat.

At my desk I was usually surrounded by three sleeping dogs at my feet. The only thing that disturbed us was the occasional delivery truck…or bear.

I look back on that time with a bit of awe. For us, it was before children. It was before 9/11, wars, pandemics, and our time of hyper-divisive politics. It was before the deaths of parents and sisters — the "everybody is alive time."

I imagine, but I do not know, that our dogs had no remembrance of our deeper past — did Riva remember our two-bedroom first-floor apartment in Minneapolis? Or Zuni and Nugie our Minnesota farmland? I also doubt they had forebodings about the future.

It's probably fair to say (again, I imagine, but do not know) that dogs and most animals aren't captured by guilt over the past and anxiety about the future. Dogs, I think, are creatures of the here and now. For example, holding a treat in my hands, thinking existential thoughts, I'm positive our dogs are not joining me in worrying about the potential of financial ruin. They are just thinking, *Throw the cookie on the floor!*

Unlike them, I am not capable of "living in the present." I was trained by my mom that the other shoe is always about to drop. To this day I spend time trying to understand the past and peer into the future. Of course, as we get older, the past looms in size while the future shrinks.

Also, to be picky, there is no such thing — technically — as the present. An archaeologist would describe "now" as the Holocene. My mom when she would yell at me to come downstairs "right now!" meant something entirely different. "Now" is not a minute or a second in time, or something you can grasp and say, "Hah! This is the present." There is only the future and then "it" immediately becomes the past.

A nerdy point, yet true.

The writer Dur e Aziz Amna wrote, "Lives should be led in the present, the eye has to look to the future, but all meaning is in the past." That is much more my style, and no meditative practice has been able to unwind me of these habits.

I will say, during the Covid pandemic, when worrying and angst seemed all about, I was taken by our dogs. They seemed to embrace the gestalt of "one day at a time." They'd arise each morning, we'd walk, they'd eat breakfast, play, take naps, play some more, and we'd do a second walk (not a lot else to do in lockdown). Evenings would go by, sitting on the couch, two dogs with their heads on my lap, and me chanting to the family, "Day by day."

Day by day. Maybe that is what meditators mean. If so, then naturally, dogs are masters of it.

Keep It Simple

───────────── ⌗ ─────────────

Another Thoreau. We have a wooden sign in our living room that has his philosophy codified: "Simplify, simplify, simplify."

Every time my father walked in and saw it, he'd grumble, "Why couldn't he simply write, 'Simplify?'"

My dad liked to cut to the chase.

Here is a lesson. Think for a minute about what makes a dog optimally happy. It is probably simple: a place to sleep, food and water, a family and guardian that cares for them, a walk or a run every day. And some off-leash freedom.

My first reaction to what a dog needs is wow! That sounds awfully right for us — us being, you know, humans. That includes the bit about off-leash freedom, even if the leash is metaphorical.

(One underlying theme of this book is get out! Go with your dog to the wilderness!)

Upon reading what a dog needs to be happy and comparing it to us, however, we all probably have an immediate reaction: Human life is much more complicated.

Work, children, schedules for work and children, time to walk the dog, parents, housing, driving in traffic, money, doctor appointments, getting laid off, a new job, a frightening illness, a grandparent dying, having to explain death to a ten-year-old while holding back tears and despair, forgetting to pay the cable bill, banishing children from social media, staying off Facebook yourself, going to a loved one's sporting events, divorces, lawyers, a parent getting dementia, standing in a grocery line and forgetting why you are there and believing that you must have dementia.

As I say, complicated, stressful.

It's easy to lose sight of the goal: to be happy; that is, content, optimistic, with maybe some joy mixed in.

The struggle is to not forget what makes us happy. I was going to go on a rant about how our current culture reinforces "busy" and acquiring things as the road to happiness, but I think we all know that is a road to emptiness.

My father often reminded me about the "tombstone test." On your tombstone, he would chide me, do you want it to read, "Here lies Hersch Wilson, he made his numbers every year" — maybe with an exclamation mark! Or, "Here lies Hersch Wilson, who followed his dreams and was happy with his life." I know that sounds binary, either/or. I have friends in the corporate world who are happy — but you get the idea.

If our goal is happiness, the way is probably a simple life. If so, our dogs, yes, those canines who are so outrageously happy to see us come home, are sentinels for simplicity.

They give us mental signals: *Take me for a walk. Rub my belly. Feed me! Life is good.*

Is It a Good Idea to Have Three Dogs and a Baby in the Wilderness?

To begin, Laurie, our dogs — Riva, Nugie, and Zuni — and I were living a simple life in the mountains next to a national forest.

We were happy, but we also had time on our hands. Maybe a bit of boredom?

So we decided to join our local volunteer fire department. In Minnesota we assumed that fire and EMS departments existed everywhere and were always a 911 call away.

Not so in New Mexico.

The motto in the rural West is, if you want something done, like quickly put out a brush fire by your house, or help someone with a broken ankle, you need to do it yourself.

We joined and went through months of training to become firefighters and EMTs (emergency medical technicians).

After about six months of calls and fire department meetings, we were integrated into that special community and having fun.

Then one night at 3 a.m. we were paged to our first house fire. Because we were still "newbies," Laurie and I spent the night hauling hoses and finding tools that were often discarded in the mud. When the fire was finally out, as the sun was coming up, the group of us stood around leaning on shovels. We were dirty and tired.

Then Laurie announced to the gathered that she was pregnant.

The chief and assistant chief, both fathers, were aghast. She had been doing hard work for hours in the middle of the night. They made her sit down on the steps of the ambulance, brought her Gatorade, and then congratulations were offered all around.

The next nine months were a blur. Doctor appointments, figuring out work, getting advice from other moms and all my sisters.

In the back of my mind, I could sense our simpler life slipping away.

Sorry, Thoreau.

One topic we skirted — what to do with the dogs? We had heard of other couples giving away their dogs when they were about to have a baby. My mom even casually asked the question, in a mom way: "So, is it a good idea to have three dogs and a new baby?"

My mother had been suspicious that we were treating our dogs like surrogate children. Oddly, in 2022, Pope Francis, looking at birth rates declining, and more young folks adopting dogs, spoke out on the same issue.

My mom was always ahead of her time.

Of course, we couldn't imagine not having dogs around. However, at night, we'd wonder, what if the dogs were hostile or became jealous? What if we started to ignore them? What if they started to snub us? Do you introduce the dogs to the baby or the baby to the dogs? A lot of our late-night musings were not exactly rational.

I'm sure that they caught on that something was

different. There were more comings and goings as we prepared the house under Laurie's, and my mom's and sisters', supervision. A lot of the dog toys were either tossed or sanitized. New furniture was moved in: crib, changing table, new couch. A bit concerned that Laurie might fall asleep while feeding the baby late at night, we broke down and bought a huge satellite dish so that Laurie could at least watch CNN while breastfeeding.

Yet the biggest change was how the dogs treated Laurie. It was as if they knew something was happening with her.

Did they know she was pregnant? Since dogs can use smell to detect bombs, cancer, and even Covid, I'm fairly certain they can detect the difference in hormonal smells as a pregnancy advances.

They were protective of her normally; now they were constantly by her side, sleeping by her feet, moving with her as she went from room to room.

A deeper dog connection with a mom-to-be? A mystery.

The day (well, the middle of the night) came, and we zoomed to the hospital leaving the dogs in the care of an "on-call" dog sitter. That was the second item on our two-page preparation list. First item: Call the moms!

Our first daughter was born, we named her Brynne Rainer, and of course, of course, I fell deeply in love.

We drove home two days later in that slow and careful way that all new parents do. I had asked for a fire department escort. The firefighters laughed and our assistant chief (a father of five) said we'd be fine.

As we arrived, the dogs came out to meet us. Laurie carefully got Brynne out of her car seat and lifted her out of the car. The three dogs gathered around curious to see and smell this new life.

As we walked into the house, I did my best to form a protective ring around Brynne and Laurie, but it wasn't necessary. The dogs were strangely calm.

Here was the singular moment that we had hoped, planned, stressed, and dreamed about.

Laurie sat down cross-legged on the floor, tightly holding Brynne, who was facing out. Then she said, "Brynne, these are our dogs." We were subtly saying to Brynne that she was coming into their house. I know that sounds completely irrational, but brand-new parents, right?

I was crouched linebacker-like, ready to pounce if anything went awry.

Nothing did.

Zuni lay down with his head on his paws and just looked at Brynne and Laurie. Riva sat down next to me, and Nugie, being Nugie, took one look and jumped up on the couch and sighed. Maybe this was because Brynne smelled like Laurie, or Laurie was so relaxed the dogs relaxed.

That's when I knew everything was going to be okay. My heart rate dropped, and I began to breathe again.

In the pictures we have of those first years, Brynne lying on a blanket, crawling, then walking, Zuni is usually in the frame. He had found his purpose, from a fun-loving German shepherd puppy to a guardian of all things Brynne. He chose to be close by her. When Brynne cried, he looked to us, expecting us to do something. He quickly learned his new role was protecting her — especially from his nemesis, the vacuum cleaner. By the time Brynne was three, she was racing Zuni up and down the hallway in our house, with Zuni always winning by an inch. When we were outside in the vegetable garden, Zuni lay in the shade, never too far away from his charge.

This is no doubt a common story, dog bonding with child, one that we might even take for granted, yet it is extraordinary.

Research has shown that when a mom looks at her child or her dog, the same brain circuitry is used. Another study found that, more than half the time, when a child moved, their dog moved with them; when the child stopped, the dog stopped.

No scientist would ever use this word, but as a writer, I

use it joyfully. It's love. If it is brain circuitry and biochemistry, who cares! It is the miracle we experience as love.

The other "miracle" is watching a child learn to love an animal. It is a vital developmental step for a child. It sets them up for a life of more compassion. Being there when a dog passes away — Brynne was three when Riva died, and one when Nugie passed — helps a child move along the road to understanding the larger picture and their role in it: empathy, strength, and kindness.

I worry that, as we shift from a primarily rural nation to an urban one (it seems inevitable), generations of kids will not have the opportunity to live with animals through birth, life, and death. Unless they have a *pet*, animals become an abstraction. (By pet, I mean preferably a dog. I suppose a cat will do. No snakes. We had friends who had a boa constrictor named Squeezy. Not a bonder.) Without exposure to animals, kids say things like eggs don't come from chickens, they come from grocery stores, as my assertive granddaughter once adamantly told me.

My sister Patty, when she was eleven and still our animal whisperer, once had to deal with Rikka having a litter of puppies in her bed at night. Rikka was only a little over a year old (*Damn you, Little Joe!* I say as I shake my fist in the air.) Patty had to help remove the amniotic sacs — in her bed — and gently massage the wet puppies until they were breathing on their own.

It sounds messy, gloppy, and gross. Patty's sheets and mattress were tossed. Yet that is the way of new life. Birth, life, sex, death are messy and gloppy — and miraculous, wonderful, and tragic.

When Brynne was six, our second miracle daughter, Sully, was born. Sully came home to a sister, parents, and two dogs, Zuni and Sombra. Zuni, as the older and now wisest shepherd, slipped back into his role of protector of all children. Sombra became the sidekick, imitating every bark, chasing after Zuni chasing balls.

Over the years, in our volumes of family pictures, we have dozens and dozens of photos of Brynne and Sully with our dogs. Pictures of two-year-olds holding sticks and the dogs patiently waiting for the girls to throw them *with all their might*. Pictures of all of them on couches, beds, lounging together on cool tile floors in the hot summer, videos of them racing down hallways to the sound of Laurie yelling at both kids and dogs to "take it outside." Later, as teenagers, horrified at being asked to pick up poop, our daughters would yell in unison, "Dad's job!" creating a carve-out from their otherwise radical feminist sensibilities.

In the back of my mind, I knew we were replicating the home that my mom created. Kids, dogs, wilderness. Laughing, crying, arguing, friends, meals, tents, sleeping bags, boyfriends who play the saxophone, soccer games, kids raiding the pantry before soccer practice, dogs on laps, dogs chasing soccer balls. Noise, parents telling kids to "hush." Kids quietly studying in their rooms with a dog on their bed.

The past is never dead, it's not even past.

Masters of What Is Important

With children, in the beginning, I was under the impression parents were the orchestrators of family life. It turns out that our dogs were the masters of that rhythm. They were the camp counselors to two often-exhausted parents. They got us up in the morning, cold snouts in our faces or jumping right on the bed. They knew when to take walks with Brynne or Sully in the jogging stroller. When it was time to play fetch, Zuni was ready with a stick, a ball, or a rock. He would bring it back to the girls and gently drop it at their feet. The dogs enforced nap times. They knew mealtimes and when the day was over, when to find their favorite spot, spin around a couple of times, scratch a blanket so it smelled like them, and then fall dead asleep. If the outside world, work, the fire department, doctor appointments, and school didn't come a calling, I think Laurie and I would've caved to their view of how life should be carried on.

Yet the outside world is a powerful sucking current that pulls you out of that warm existence.

It is like the time when your whole family, dogs included, are all snuggled in the same bed, a blizzard pounding away outside. You are comfortable and warm, then the fire department pager rings and you must go. Or you need to catch a plane to god-knows-where for work, and you must go. Or against every fiber of your being, as the snow pounds down, you must get the kids up to go to school.

In those moments, Zuni and Sombra, nestled on the bed, looked up at us in confusion. They seemed to be thinking: *You don't get it. All that outside world stuff is interesting and occasionally humans must submit, but life is here. A family altogether, warm, fed, as a storm hammers the windows.*

Is there some deep social instinct in a dog that "knows," when the pack is together, those are the most cherished of times? Do we, too, know this deep in our thinking: What is most essential is a family together as the storm rages?

We are taught by culture that we "must" get up and go, whatever the storm may bring. Ignore nature, they tell us. Ignore the warmth, the moaning of still-dream-entranced children.

We are taught that "perfect attendance" in school prepares us for "perfect attendance" on the factory line. The world won't efficiently work, profits will not grow, without perfect attendance.

Yet living in the wilderness, in the foothills above Santa Fe, with dogs and children, those rules seem less important. There is a different rhythm, a deeper perspective on what is important — and it is not perfect attendance. There are days when the best thing you can do is to tell your children — because they get anxious about missing school — that today is a special magical day. Today, we are going to listen to our dogs. We are going to watch the snow blow or harvest vegetables from the garden or just read Harry Potter together. A quiet revolt. A soft questioning of the status quo. The next morning, we will write notes to school saying that our children needed a mental health day. Or, if we are truly brave, we will write that it was a special magical day, and the dogs requested our presence.

Zuni Just Wants to Run

It is also magical when you live in the mountains with an unleashed dog who wants to run.

Zuni was insistent that a day not go by without a run. He was the best fitness partner ever.

He'd stare at me in the morning when I was still sleeping, his chin on our bed and tail wagging, waiting for me to open my eyes. If that didn't work, by lunchtime he'd be in the office with his head on my lap. Finally, if it was midafternoon and we hadn't run, he would sit in the kitchen and bark.

Mornings were our favorite times. Even in high summer, at seven thousand feet it was still cool. We took off, Zuni sprinting ahead and circling back to assure I was still coming.

We ran on our road for half a mile and then cut onto a trail that led to the mountains. I galumphed along as Zuni zigzagged back and forth, making sure not to miss anything; new smells, maybe hightailing after that near-mythical jackrabbit.

About three feet wide, the first part of the trail rose gently. It's an area where multiple branches of trails braid from the plains toward the ancient Arroyo Hondo Pueblo (1400 BCE) and Santa Fe, ten miles to the north. Underneath Santa Fe are the ruins of the Ogapogee Pueblo, translated as "the White Shell Water Place."

Every time we were on this trail, Zuni set our pace while I pondered this history. I imagined Indigenous peoples using this same trail, the Anasazi, the Pueblo, and later, occasionally, an Apache raiding party. The fourteenth-century Pueblo Alamo lies three miles directly west, abandoned in the sixteenth century because of fire and drought, then destroyed in 1971 by construction of the I-25 interstate. (Progress, progress.) I often spotted artifacts, pieces of pottery, obsidian arrowheads and flakes, as I ran these trails.

Once Laurie and I spent a day (it was a birthday present) with an archaeologist just walking around the ranch where Laurie worked. He pointed out old eighteenth-century hacienda foundations, ancient middens, nineteenth-century garbage dumps, pottery — a list of artifacts that we'd walked over and never seen. He told us that when you're trained as an archaeologist, you never see geography in the same way. History and prehistory are everywhere.

The Pueblo people had dogs. The aforementioned Arroyo Hondo was excavated by the Santa Fe School for Advanced Research (aka, the Glorious Nerds of Santa Fe), where they found skeletal remains of dogs inside structures, though some researchers think the remains might be domesticated coyotes.

Again, all conclusions are "provisional approximations."

They used dogs to hunt, and dogs were scavengers, getting rid of food waste. They were used in rituals (often killed and buried in ceremonies) and as food. For over twelve thousand years, dogs lived with the region's Indigenous peoples, and as Zuni and I ran the trail, I always envisioned those ancient dogs and their humans running together on a hunt.

At a particular scree slope, Zuni usually loped up until he was out of sight, leaving me to scramble to the top. Yet there he always was, waiting for me.

He was patient. He never got too far ahead or headed off on his own.

We ran through the piñon forests and climbed into the ponderosa and rock outcroppings of the ancient Rockies. Then, both of us panting, we climbed the next slope and stopped.

To the west, Sandia Peak towered over Albuquerque. North were the peaks of the Sangre de Cristos, named by the Spanish explorer Valverde y Cosío in 1719 because, apparently, the sun setting turned the snow-covered peaks red and reminded him of "the blood of Christ." To the east, below the ridge we lived on, was an old Confederate Civil War encampment (the Battle of Glorieta Pass was the westernmost battle of the war). Farther out was the Pecos Wilderness and the Pecos River valley, where you can still find wagon tracks from the nineteenth-century Santa Fe Trail. South were the plains of Galisteo. Our house, on the ridgeline, was only possible because of electricity to power our well and provide heat. If the grid ever melts down, that house will eventually turn into a warren for animals, and then dust. The village of Galisteo, constructed more sensibly in the basin of the Rio Galisteo, has been occupied for centuries.

History and lessons everywhere.

Each time, hands on my head, breathing hard, we'd both take in the view and the moment. I'd look at Zuni, and he'd look back, wondering if we were going to run until dark or turn and go home.

I imagined both of us thinking the same thing. We could do this forever. We ran through the snows in winter, climbing over snowdrifts, and the thunderstorms of August — racing to get home in pouring rain and thunder. This was where we belonged.

Some days we continued. Just another thirty minutes. Just until we could see snow atop Santa Fe Baldy, towering over Santa Fe at twelve thousand feet. Zuni never seemed to tire. Some days his spirit was infectious. I grew up running. My dad grabbed me as a running partner when I was fifteen (and lazy). I learned to love it and spent lots of mornings and evenings out on roads running alone or with our family dogs. On roads it's hard to let your mind wander: traffic and other people. Lots of distractions. The asphalt I ran on was hard and unforgiving.

Running with Zuni in the wild was a wholly different experience. The surface was pine needles, sand, and dirt. There were no people.

When your breath matches your stride, the air is cool, and a dog is ahead of you setting the pace, running is almost effortless, floating. On long runs it was as if we were connected, thinking the same thoughts, feeling the freedom, loving the sense of hard breathing and muscles and tendons getting stronger every stride.

Sometimes, after reaching the highest point of the run, we'd sit down together and catch our breath. I'd scratch him behind his ears, and he'd lie down, tongue out, cooling off. I liked to imagine that he was, like me, content. We were alone in the wild. We had stripped off the comfortable ways of civilization and felt, at least in that moment, lean and fit, able to thrive out here.

On morning runs, we started down toward home before the sun rose too high. Running downhill was a race with us. Going downhill, gravity is your friend. Zuni ran alongside me, getting in front or behind only when the trail narrowed. My arms went up in the air as we slid down the scree slope. Then, as the trail flattened out, we both slowed down. Neither of us were ever quite ready to be back. It was the tug of mountains, nature's Sphinxes and Mona Lisas, the river-polished stone, the quiet with just our breathing for sound, my head still spinning through thousands of years of history. Zuni just wanted to run. Slouching into the driveway, Sombra (when still a puppy) came and greeted us and jumped up on me. Zuni went straight to the water dish on the front steps.

We all went into the house together. Zuni did his perimeter check to make sure everything was on the up-and-up and then headed for the couch for a postrun nap.

Now decades later, I walk with our dogs. As an older human, I have a few "stupidity-caused orthopedic injuries," my term for my history of doing things that begin with thinking, *What's the worst that can happen?* Turns out injuries to knees, ankles, wrists, brain, and hands can, and do, happen.

Even though I enjoy walking our dogs, it just isn't the same as a mountain trail with Zuni running ahead of me. *Exhilaration* is the word I'm looking for. Sitting on the floor, lacing up running shoes with Zuni next to me whining, ready to go. Opening the door, getting hit with a blast of cool autumn air, seeing him leap off the steps and start with a sprint. The feel of those first steps, as my breathing caught up, wondering if this will be a hard run or a floating one — Zuni always seemed to float.

Everything in my being says we are meant to run. Our ancestors, long-distance runners, chased down prey. It is in our genes; it is who we are, how we are built. The arches in our feet, the length of our Achilles tendons, our ability to sweat. We've been running for two million years.

When Zuni was in deep nap stage, he slept sidewise on the couch. His paws hung over the edge of the couch, twitching as he dreamed. I imagined him dreaming of our runs. I do. Even later in life, with Zuni gone, older, and no longer living in that house tucked in the forest, I dream. I dream of the trees bending over us, the smell of piñon, the crunch of ancient gravel and scree, the boulders and snow-drifts that we navigated around. I can see Zuni loping, looking back at me with that dog smile.

Coyote Fit

———⟨∽⟩———

Here is the lesson: Your dog should look like a healthy coyote.

Let me explain.

Zuni was a hyperactive German shepherd. He once jumped off a second-story deck to chase me when I took off on a fire department call. He almost caught me, and I was going nearly thirty miles an hour. He was a lean dog. When I petted him, I could feel his ribs. This turns out to be an important sign.

We've had two dogs — to our shame because it was our fault — who were clinically obese. Nugie, our collie, and Tank, one of our Bernese mountain dogs, were both "fat" for dogs.

The fact is, we have a dog obesity crisis, not only in this country, but worldwide. Depending on sources, 30 to 50 percent of domestic dogs are obese. Dogs are considered obese when they are 20 percent over their ideal body weight.

Our veterinarian at the time, Dr. Timothy Byrne of the Eldorado Animal Clinic, remarked that obesity is the most devastating health problem that he deals with on a regular basis. Dogs, he went on, will "eat themselves to death." They will continue to eat and gain weight, causing heart and kidney disease, arthritis, and metabolic obesity — where fat tends to congregate around organs in the body, diminishing their function.

Studies have shown that obese dogs have reduced life expectancy and mobility. Overweight dogs are basically in a constant state of inflammation, predisposing them to more severe osteoarthritis and chronic diseases.

The other point that Dr. Byrne made, which I thought was intriguing, was that our perception of what a healthy dog looks like is mostly wrong. We've grown accustomed to seeing slightly "fat" dogs as normal.

He said that we should look to the coyote — thin, lean, and fit — as a better example of what a dog should naturally look like. As I could with Zuni, if you can feel the ribs of an otherwise healthy dog, they are probably at the right weight.

How we help our dogs stay "coyote thin" is by — old news — reducing their total calories and keeping them active. That means making the daily run or walk a priority.

CHILDHOOD IS THE KINGDOM
WHERE NO ONE EVER DIES

Zuni passed away suddenly. We had temporarily relocated back to Minnesota for a two-year work stint. We had a big yard but no fence. Zuni got out of the house, chased a car, and was hit and killed by another vehicle. Laurie ran down to the road and I heard her keen and wail as she held him.

I had never heard that sound before. It still haunts.

So this brings us to the sad yet necessary part of this book: Our dogs die before us.

Let me begin with a movie.

When I watched *Old Yeller*, the classic Disney movie, for the first time, I was nine and we were in a theater. That probably constrained my reaction to the ending a bit, plus even then I understood the role of men was to not show emotion, at least not in public. But I betcha I cried in the car on the way home.

A generation flies by. The movie *Old Yeller* hasn't changed. And neither has the reaction of, at least, our children.

I learned the hard way. As a parent, having overcome the fact that Yeller is shot, I thought a family movie night showing the Disney classic would be a hit with our daughters, then age eleven and five.

I was wrong. When Travis lifts the gun to face a snarling Yeller, our daughters bolted from the room. A sleepless night for the parents ensued as both daughters had night-mares.

I understand the point Disney is making in its movies. From *Bambi* to *Dumbo* to *The Lion King*, death or suffering precedes a somewhat happy ending. The point being, life is hard, and you need to be ready. To that point, Bruno Bettelheim, the Austrian psychologist who specialized in autism, thought the Grimm fairy tales (which are grim) should not be sanitized for young children.

Yet try telling those fairy tales or explaining why Travis had to kill Yeller to twenty-first-century young children — it doesn't go over well.

There is something about sad animal movies that just strikes a chord with our children. Adults can die, no problem. Take *Jurassic Park*. When the lawyer in the outhouse is eaten by the *Tyrannosaurus rex*, our kids ate their popcorn. (I want to note here, for the record, that our family doesn't have an anti-attorney bias; he was just a "grown-up.") When the dinosaur wrangler says, "Clever girl," right before he is killed by the velociraptor, both girls thought it was a great movie line — now Brynne has it as a bumper sticker on her car. Yet when the goat is eaten by the *T. rex*, that caused consternation. Sully argued on the way home that the goat had "magically" broken the rope around their neck and escaped.

When both our daughters were in their teens, we saw the movie *Homeward Bound*, about two dogs and a cat in the wilderness trying to find a way back to their human family. Shadow, the old and wise golden retriever, falls in a pit when they are almost home. At precisely that moment, Brynne, our oldest and in high school at the time, bolted from her seat and ran out of the theater. I had to follow her and explain that Shadow gets out of the pit and is reunited with his human family.

Once, we were in a theater for a nondog movie. As we sat down, we were confronted with a preview for the film *A Dog's Purpose*, in which, apparently, five dogs live full lives, pass on, and yet possess a single purpose and soul they share through all their lives.

Tears and anxiety in our row. Sully, fourteen at the time, whispered to me, almost sobbing, "Five dogs *die*? I'm never going to see that!"

Movies were reinforcing the life lesson: Their dogs will die, and it is painful. Their early response was to have nothing to do with anything that reminded them of that, be it Old Yeller or the *Jurassic Park* goat.

And yet reality crashed on them too soon. It is always too soon; you can be thirty and it is too soon.

In 2003, Brynne was fifteen and Sully was nine when Sombra developed incurable liver cancer. She was in pain and had trouble moving. Anytime we approached her, she wagged her tail in greeting, but that was about all she could do.

Laurie and I took her to the vet and determined it was time. In past generations, the decision would probably have been to just get it over with, to not expose the kids to this. Laurie, however, did not want to cheat them out of saying goodbye to Sombra. This also meant that they would be there when she died.

Laurie went to the schools and picked up both girls so they could sit with Sombra in her last minutes. The girls were a bit afraid and trepidatious at first, yet also knew that they wanted to say goodbye to Sombra. Sombra had her head on Laurie's lap as the vet gave her the injections, one for pain and one to put her to sleep. We all sat with a hand on her and cried.

The poet Edna St. Vincent Millay wrote, "Childhood is the kingdom where no one ever dies." It is a kingdom that never lasts. Growing up means understanding and accepting that death, even the death of a dog, is part of living.

The singularly hardest part of living is accepting death, of family, friends, and dogs, and then continuing to live and find joy. When I think of important stuff that dogs teach us, this is the most salient if painful lesson.

Our kids of course were devastated when Sombra stopped breathing. It is so hard to confront death. I helped the vet wrap Sombra and bring her in the back office, where she would be cremated. Then, I came back, and we all just held each other and continued to cry.

I had to repeat to our children and remind myself: It isn't that dogs die. That is inevitable and out of our control. What is important is that we live with them. That we have time with them.

As long as they are alive, day after day, they are with us. That is to be celebrated. We have dog birthdays. My nephew and niece had a Bark Mitzvah for their dog, Leo.

We will die and must celebrate life. Our loved ones will die, and we must celebrate life. Our dogs will die, and we must celebrate life.

The other lesson, which just seems to be how life works, is that we often need to experience death, sometimes the death of someone close to us, be it human or dog, to understand any of this. Cast larger, this is one of the great paradoxes of living. We can't know true joy until we've been through the valley of the shadow.

In Ecclesiastes it's written, "There is a time to mourn and a time to dance." They are not separate and distinct; rather, they are part of the whole, threads of the same woven cloth. We mourn, we grieve, we sing, and we dance.

DOG LESSON
Zoomies

On the rare occasions that it happens, we feel a sense of exhilaration, a deep sense of enjoyment that is long cherished and that becomes a landmark in memory for what life should be like. This is what we mean by "optimal experience."

— MIHALY CSIKSZENTMIHALYI

In Santa Fe, I'm happy when at the end of the day our garden hasn't wilted away because of the summer heat and drought. I feel joy when a rare thunderstorm, a monsoonal downpour, hits us, the temperature drops from the nineties to under sixty, and I can stand in our garage and watch torrential rain wash the dust and smoke out of the sky and change everything. Or, after weeks of hot and dry, I can stand under our drain spouts (canales) and get soaked.

It's a high-desert thing.

Maisie, our Chihuahua mix, every once in a while, with no warning, will begin jumping from couch to chair and back again.

Zoomies!

If our daughter Sully holds one of Maisie's toys, they will play tug. Then Toby will join in, and they will play-growl, tug, and chase until Maisie slips under a table to rest. They are happy when they are fed, and we go on walks. They seem joyful when they play.

Why don't we, every once in a while, experience the pure ecstasy of zoomies?

It begins with perspective. I am not sure if dogs have a long-term memory that grants them perspective. Yet Maisie, I think, is joyful because of her past. Before we adopted her, she was a street dog. A difficult life. Now, through twists and turns, she's with us. She is loved and we take care of her. For the first time in her life, she doesn't have to worry about eating, being left alone, not knowing who her humans are, or feeling secure. She can play. She can be joyful.

For us, joy — the standing-under-the-canales-in-the-rain-dancing-zoomies joy — begins with the truly astonishing fact that on this day, whatever day it is, we are alive. In this astonishingly large, empty, and ancient universe, we are alive, it is our sweet and wonderful time. As you read this, you are alive. It is easy to lose that perspective, what with our illusory assumption that we will live a long time.

Yet even sometimes when the rain is pouring outside, after weeks of dry, we hesitate. We think, *We're grown-ups.* We are more comfortable on the sidelines of experience. Let the kids go dance in the rain, and splash in the puddles, while we hold a coffee cup in our hands, lists in our minds, and watch out for lightning. It is hard for us to let go and get wet. However, if we do not, if we cut ourselves off from "optimal experiences," from ecstatic moments, we risk becoming old and crotchety. (The pull to be old and crotchety is always there.)

These moments reveal themselves if we pay attention.

Once, at my nephew's wedding, a group spontaneously began dancing the hora. It was loud, there was drinking, and we were happy. (How glorious is a wedding!) I stood and watched, with my arms crossed. Suddenly, before I could think and politely refuse, someone grabbed my hand and pulled me into the circle of delirious celebrants. Around we went. I lost track of who I was. I was no longer "me." I was a Dancer, joining a thousands-of-years-old tradition of dancing at weddings. I lost track of time and movement. Like Maisie, ecstatically jumping from couch to couch, I was all in. "Dance," Rumi wrote, "where you can break yourself up to pieces and totally abandon your worldly passions."

Be greedy for those moments!

If you need a mental picture to remind you of this, of joy and exhilaration, see a happy and smiling dog running, diving into mud pools, shaking themselves dry. Everything you need to know about joy, about "optimal experience," is right there. Zoom on!

Part 4

Life with Berners!

Once you have had a wonderful dog,
a life without one is a life diminished.

— Dean Koontz, *A Big Little Life:*
A Memoir of a Joyful Dog Named Trixie

After our two-year stint in Minnesota, we moved back to New Mexico. As much as we loved living at the end of a three-mile dirt road next to the wilderness, we decided that, now with kids, responding to fire department calls, and Laurie's new job in town, we should live closer to Santa Fe and on a real, asphalt road. I could rhapsodize about the pleasures of asphalt after living on a car-destroying neighborhood-maintained road, but that would be anti–Santa Fean. Dirt roads are part of the mystique.

After Zuni and Sombra passed away, it took us a while to even think about getting another dog. A month or two went by in our new house and it felt different. No dogs wrestling. No barking. No dogs' heads on laps in the evening.

We began missing and thinking about dogs, but aspects of our lives had changed. We were older, we had one preteen and one teenage daughter, and now their friends were constantly at our house. As a warning note to parents of athletes, it's astonishing how much a girls soccer team can eat after school. Boys eat just the offered pizza. Girls eat everything in the pantry. They are locusts.

Because of all the comings and goings, we decided that we needed a dog that was a little less "protective" than our German shepherds — less likely to plow through a screen window to be with us, as Sombra had done.

We also wanted a BIG DOG. This would have serious ramifications, like being towed on walks, yet at the time we weren't thinking ahead. Not thinking ahead is a genetic condition that both Laurie and I apparently inherited. Once, in the eighties, my brother Joey had agonized over buying an Apple Lisa Computer. I told him to get it because it would probably be the last computer he would ever buy. Thinking ahead: not a skill.

The dog that fit the bill, after Laurie researched innumerable breeds, was the Bernese mountain dog. We had reservations. Big purebreds often come with a host of genetically caused illnesses that can shorten their lives, and big dogs have short lives to begin with. There was also a burgeoning awareness in our family of the plight of shelter dogs. That question hung over us. We asked ourselves, shouldn't we adopt a dog from the shelter? We had lots of conversations about all of this, some even on the way out to just "visit" a litter of Bernese mountain dog puppies.

I remember that Sully, our radical animal rights advocate, was making the shelter argument (for the nth time) as we walked up to the house and into the living room. As we greeted the human Berner "mom," Sully had her arms crossed and was not giving up. In an unfair attempt to sway the argument, the woman let a swarm of eight-week-old Berner puppies into the room. Emotional manipulation. And it worked. When you are sitting on the floor being licked and jumped on by Berner puppies, logical arguments simply fly away, never to be regained. It was love at first sight and puppy joy. And so we entered the happy chaos of Berner-hood.

Enjoy Chaos? Adopt
Bernese Mountain Dog Puppies

Our first Berner was a male named Oso ("bear" in Spanish). Even as a puppy, he exhibited wild and woolly characteristics. One morning, sitting in the kitchen having coffee, I heard Sully yelling, "He's in the living room and he's got something big!"

I walked in and watched Oso throw around one of Sully's life-size stuffed animals: tossing it in the air and catching it. A couple of times he tossed it and knocked over a chair and then demolished a standing lamp. Seeing me, he jumped into "play position" and sprinted away into Brynne's room. Yelling ensued as he did the unthinkable: wake up a teenager on a Saturday morning.

It continued. Another time, I heard Sully yell, "Cuteness is not a superpower!" as she was chased down the hallway by Oso. Sully sprinted into her room and closed the door. Oso began jumping on the door, scratching, and yapping to get in. He was using Konrad Lorenz's "baby schema" for evil.

Remember the scene in the original *Jurassic Park* where Laura Dern gets chased by velociraptors, barely makes it into the computer room, and the velociraptors get their claws in the crack of the door? Also, her memorable cry to her compatriots: *"Run!"* Life with a Berner puppy is like that. We also attempted the "freeze and be still" idea from the same movie — holding our breaths and standing motionless in the kitchen — to no avail. Dogs aren't *T. rexes*. They don't need motion to track prey, and they will hunt you down to play.

After we adopted Oso, we had two or three Berners in our home for the next fifteen years. There was Oso, Mowgli, Jamaica, and finally Tank and Nellie, our last pair of Berners. Our daughters, Sully and Brynne, lived from 2003 to 2018 with Berners constantly demanding their attention and love. Here are some of the things we learned....

There are four stages to a Berner's life. Cute puppyhood, then they morph into velociraptors, then a mature and more laid-back stage, and then old age (which you pray will last more than a couple of years).

Cute puppyhood seems to pass in a matter of days. The velociraptor stage takes ages.

Witness: At two years old, Oso learned to surprise attack by jumping over the back of a couch and landing on your lap. At eighty pounds, it could be quite a shock. Nellie, at the same age, destroyed every soccer ball and inflatable exercise ball in the house. And not as you would think, while we were away, but right in front of me. She was daring me to stop her. Tank got his name because at ten weeks he sprinted into a wall headfirst, bounced off, *and was fine.*

In puppy school, Mowgli was a star pupil, calm, obedient, and happy to learn. He was going to be a grade-school reading buddy but passed away at five.

Our most dramatic couple, Tank and Nellie, took the same puppy-school class a few years later. They were not calm, nor obedient, and wanted nothing to do with learning.

Nellie couldn't care less about treats — nothing motivated her to sit, heel, or stop barking. Tank, subservient to Nellie, just sat at the end of the puppy line and barked. Finally, the trainer asked us to leave the class or get private lessons. They both got Fs on their permanent records. This was the second time a dog, I mean me, had failed in puppy class.

Our Berners were walkers, not runners. I was thankful for it because I was getting older, and my knees were showing their age. Yet Tank wouldn't even walk in the beginning. He would manage to get down the driveway, turn on to our road, and immediately lie down and roll over on his back. A forty-pound puppy is an immovable object. We would beg and offer treats — he'd take the treats and lie right back down.

My only descriptive analog is when a young child has a temper tantrum in a grocery store, and you end up dragging them along the floor until they're embarrassed and get up. Only Tank never got embarrassed. He was content just watching the sky from his upside-down, splayed out, puppy position.

When all of our Berners were young, we tried crating them at night so that we could sleep and not worry about nocturnal destruction. Mowgli liked the crate; it was his "man cave."

The rest had nothing to do with it. They howled as if being cruelly treated. We tried the put-the-crate-as-far-away-from-us-as-possible method. Didn't help. We could still hear them. In bed, Laurie and I reassured each other that they were fine. Eventually, the kids came into our room at night and pleaded with us to "do something." We tried the crate-in-our-bedroom method, so we could soothe them. Nope. They always knew we were near the breaking point. Nellie and Tank were especially adept at this. They would've made great police detectives; their barking and whining would've broken anyone. "I confess! Just please, please, make the dogs stop barking!"

Yes, we capitulated. We let them out of their crates, and they jumped on the beds, turned a couple of dog circles to mess up the sheets, and collapsed down, falling asleep with big victory sighs.

Outside the house, we kept leashes on our Berners lest mayhem arise. Nellie off-leash was always gone like a shot, cruising the neighborhood. I'd get three or four calls from neighbors that Nellie had dropped by and could I come get her.

Once, I mistimed holding the leashes and opening the garage door (rookie mistake). I opened the door, Mowgli and Jamaica sensed freedom, saw two other little dogs on a walk with their humans, and the race was on. The other dogs were terrified and took off. I was running and yelling at them to come back and trying to reassure the humans that they just wanted to play. All the dogs were fine, the humans not so much. I had to apologize with deep remorse. I tried to explain the velociraptor concept to no avail.

Every aspect of our daily and nightly life was influenced — controlled? orchestrated? managed? — by the Berners. For example, how long could we be gone without re-creating the Great Wallpaper Incident with Zuni? Three hours seemed about the maximum amount of time. This led to critical schedule discussions each morning: Who would be home and by when? It was also recognized that Berners were the most crazed for the first few minutes after we left. Once, I came home within ten minutes because I'd forgotten something. I found Nellie and Tank destroying some of their toys — fluff all over the living room.

Further — not that we were highly social — but having insane Berners put a damper on having adult company at our house. The soccer kids loved the Berners. They didn't mind getting jumped on and would play with them for hours: kids and dogs.

We could only have guests who were prequalified to handle the jumping, the barking, the sitting on your lap. One of my favorite memories of that time is of a friend sitting on a couch, Berner on her lap and a drink in her hand. All I could see was two arms, a drink, and a large and affectionate dog.

The portal to much of this craziness was — and is — our front door. I am pretty sure that biology and genetics aside, dogs are hardwired to react to knocking, the doorbell, or the wind blowing against a front door.

I dreamed once that there was a circle of dogs sitting in front of said door. A dog instructor was pointing out the number of ways a dog could open an unlocked door (yes, it has been done), how to tell the difference between the sounds squirrels, delivery folks, and random humans make. At the end, all the dogs raised a paw and swore to defend the door at all costs.

To deflect the militaristic enthusiasm of Berners to slobber on anyone or anything coming through the front door, we did everything that trainers suggested. We stationed treats by the door. This demonstrated to us one of the most frightening aspects of dogs: Some care not about treats. With some of our canines, we used hot dogs, and they were not distracted from their mission of alerting us that someone was on the other side of the door!

We practiced knocking and coming in and out of the door, so they were attenuated to it. Nope. They could tell the difference between our efforts and a real-live other person.

On those rare occasions when we had friends over, the drill went something like this:

First, everyone knew to call us first (much like the sign in my family's driveway growing up). No surprise visits. When the Jehovah's Witnesses showed up unannounced, it was wild, and a couple of non-JW-like words were uttered.

With that knowledge, Laurie and I, or the girls, assembled at the door because it took more than one person to manage the situation. Then, after letting our friends in, we decided: Either a) put the Berners outside in the back fenced yard (although that caused an uproar of barking and scratching on doors that made conversation virtually impossible) or b) keep the dogs with us. On hopeful days, we let them get to know our friends to see what would happen. Usually that meant Laurie and I holding dogs and collars while explaining that the dogs wouldn't bite; they were just *enthusiastic*, and slobbery.

An abandoned strategy, attempted only a few times, was to put them in a bedroom and hope for the best. Why abandoned? First, howling dogs seemed to lead our guests to think we were punishing them. Second, *our dogs learned how to open doors*. Once this happened, Laurie and I were no longer listening to our guests talk; we were keenly focused on hearing a door lever being turned and a door creaking open. (I eventually had to change all our door openers from levers to knobs.)

When a door opened, Laurie and I immediately assumed what any basketball player would recognize as a defensive position: down low, knees soft and bent, and positioned sideways to absorb the coming blow and not let the dogs pass.

Our guests, even the ones who knew our dogs, were a bit startled by the sight of two or three dogs storming down the hallway wanting to be the center of attention.

Further, Berners, like our current Great Pyrenees, Toby, have this deep and reverberating bark designed to terrify. Once a nice and creative electric meter guy left us a note saying he was afraid to go to the back of the house because he could hear "Cujo" barking at him from in the garage. I totally understood his point of view. Of course, "Cujo," aka Oso, immediately left the garage, found our daughter doing homework in the living room, pushed all the books away, and lay contentedly by her.

So fierce!

A final note about biting: Were Laurie and I being honest when we told our friends that our giant Berners didn't bite? Yes and no. There are almost 4.5 million reported incidents of dogs biting humans each year. One in five individuals bitten by dogs needs medical attention. A dog bite can have a force of over 250 psi. For perspective, humans have a bite force of about 80 psi, and our bites are often much more infectious than animal bites (lots of gross bacteria).

Any dog can bite if provoked, but our dogs never did. What they were guilty of was nipping. A nip is not a full-on bite, which you know when it happens. Nipping is often done playfully or when a dog gets excited. Here, I take full blame; our dogs were not really the guilty parties. I have always played rough-and-tumble, chasing games with our dogs. Sometimes they have grabbed my shirt to hang on to me. The German shepherds used to take my arm — gently — in their mouths and guide me to wherever they wanted to go. Sometimes our games of tug-of-war got out of hand — we loved to play all over the house, diving off furniture, wrestling. As a result, I am still known for wearing lots of Band-Aids. When I admitted this to a trainer once, he bluntly told me that I was teaching them, *Nipping is fun! Go for it! Even Hersch's mom! Yay!*

With our dogs, including our Berners, we have had occasional front-door, excited-dog incidents of nipping. The most infamous was when my brother Joey (a dog person) burst through our front door when Zuni was dead asleep next to it. Zuni jumped up, barked, and nipped. This is the genesis of the saying, "Let sleeping dogs lie." At Laurie's insistence, I apologized, but come on. He grew up in a house with the sign "Don't get out of your car!" He shoulda known...

Let the Dogs Out,
Let the Dogs In…

One of the great causes of disruption in a house with dogs is the dog's schedule. This is doubled or tripled depending on the number of dogs.

In our kitchen we have a sign that describes life with dogs: "Agenda for the day: Let the dogs out, let the dogs in, let the dogs out, let the dogs in."

After years of this, of conversations being interrupted to put a dog in or out, Laurie and I stumbled across one of the greatest inventions of modern dog guardianship.

I don't know about you, but I had no idea I needed an iPhone until Apple invented it. That is the point of innovation, coming up with things that we can't imagine, and they become the stuff of our day-to-day lives, stuff we can't live without, stuff we crave.

But the iPhone is not the greatest invention in our view. It is not the invention that created more time, more convenience, or allowed us to be essentially lazy on a Sunday morning. That honor, my friends, goes to the dog door.

With the Berners, going in and out was an every-half-hour thing. They had to patrol the perimeter of their fenced yard eight times a day. Some went out just to check on the weather and come right back in. Nellie insisted on being outside especially if there were gale-like winds and snow.

They all had different peeing and pooping schedules. Of course, if a coyote had the temerity to howl close to our house, day or night, all the dogs needed to be let out to bark. Not to do anything productive, just bark.

Our first solution was to have our kids oversee letting the dogs in and out. Then school got in the way. Worse, teenage daughters have this unique talent of rolling their eyes when you politely ask them to do anything, and they always had a mom to back them up. "I have too much homework." "I have to sleep." "I don't want to!" "No."

It is astonishing really, and a testament to me being a slow adopter, that it took me three decades to figure out this time-saving innovation. We had been a dog-centric family, yet we had overlooked this most important item.

The problem had existed since I was ten with our first dog, Shawnee. Our house eventually had eight individual humans living in it, all of whom had perfected the ability to ignore a dog whining and assume that someone else would let her out or in.

Shawnee would leave deep scratches in the door (as if telling us, *Put a dog door here!*) and occasionally a little present that would cause holy hell and yet another family meeting if my dad stepped in it. The rest of us were quite adroit about avoiding and ignoring Shawnee's, or any dog's, poop.

We were just not on the ball innovation-wise. In retrospect, if our family had lived during the fourth century BCE, we would have been content to drag stuff around on sticks rather than fall for that newfangled invention, the wheel.

Laurie's and my revelation — and it was almost a religious awakening in the sense that it shook our understanding of how the universe could work — came when we had lunch with another couple who had three dogs. They casually mentioned having to close their dog door at night because their dogs would go out, start barking, and bug their neighbors.

Laurie and I looked at each other and *finally* the lightbulb blinked on.

A dog door!

It got even better. Our friend was a carpenter, and he told us that he could put in a dog door in our house.

At that moment, understanding the implications of what that could mean nearly caused me to weep.

Joyfully, we said yes. We were silent on the way home as we ruminated about how our lives were about to change.

A week later we bashed a square hole in a wall by our back door and put in a lovely dog door that opened into a fenced yard.

And as could be expected, the dogs completely ignored it. I think they liked the power they had over us: *Let them out, let them in, let them out…*

Nellie and Tank were our "experimental" dogs. It took a lot of coaxing to get Nellie to try it. (She was, like me, not a first adopter.) We held the door open, and she'd look at it suspiciously. We used treats to no avail. The breakthrough came when Tank — seeing a treat — bashed through the door, reinforcing why he was named Tank. Nellie, upon seeing this, gently nosed the door open and stepped through. Success!

Within days, our lives changed. Now, we could sit in the kitchen in the morning, drink coffee, and listen to the sweet music of the dog door opening and swinging closed: *Dogs going out, dogs coming in, dogs going out…*

Once they had learned it, they passed on the knowledge of the greatest home invention to subsequent dogs. It was a perfect system!

Believe it or not, there are trainers who discourage dog doors. They warn that it cedes too much power to dogs. They like the idea of a dog having to ask to go in or out. It reinforces the pecking order in the house.

They are wrong.

Countervailing evidence: a full night's sleep. Not having to get up early to let the dogs out and stand there half-asleep when it's freezing while they pee. Not being able to focus for more than a few minutes because dogs are constantly interrupting when you are writing the greatest novel in the history of novels, which after a week of dog in / dog out reads like a fifth-grade version of *Ulysses*. (As a note, James Joyce's wife, Nora, after reading the first part of *Ulysses*, asked him if he could write something people could read. Maybe he had a dog that he was constantly letting in and out.)

But there is a caveat or two. The first is raccoons. They are devilish and often scary animals. Do not be misguided by their cuteness.

Once, while staying at my mother's home in Minnesota when our kids were young, we were all sleeping in an upstairs bedroom. We heard a noise outside and all of us went to the window. There was a raccoon standing on top of a bird feeder. I opened the window and yelled at him (or her) to get off. The raccoon reared up and hissed at me. A loud and angry hiss. I slammed the second-story window shut. The girls were wide-eyed.

Raccoons will figure out a dog door and get in your house. This is bad. As will squirrels if you have them.

Back in New Mexico, we had a mountain lion bang her head on our sliding glass door in our kitchen once, but she did not jump over our courtyard wall, which she could have easily done, and find our dog door. A mountain lion in the house would have been catastrophic, as in millions-of-views-on-YouTube catastrophic. (Our daughter Sully would've videoed the entire event and added music.)

As fortune has it, we don't have many raccoons, we're home to one squirrel who keeps to himself, and the mountain lion was — we hope — an isolated incident.

I suppose if you live in Florida, snakes and other assorted reptiles might also pose a problem. There was a story about a Florida man getting up at 5 a.m. to take a shower. Half-awake, he opened the shower door to find a six-foot boa constrictor curled on the floor. No mention of blood-curdling screaming; I think that was edited out of the report. The snake had slithered in through the dog door. Maybe if you live in Florida, forget this entire chapter.

But aren't those just details compared to the tranquility of sitting in your kitchen, having coffee, and listening to the sweet swinging sound of a dog door?

I rest my case.

Escaping

I admit here to a bias. As a teenager, I spent a lot of time pondering the question, why do dogs want to escape? As the oldest, it was my job to respond to neighbors' calls that our boarded horses or our dogs were out. Those calls usually came early in the morning. It began with my mom yelling from downstairs, "Herschel! The horses (or dogs) are at the Browns!" In a way it was good preparation for being a firefighter: I developed the ability to get out of bed, get dressed, jump into a car, and drive to a "scene" while still basically asleep. With horses, they got out usually because someone left a gate open. I'd find them contentedly grazing in a neighbor's vegetable garden. With dogs, they'd most often be in a pack of other dogs chasing deer or just randomly barking at a house. *Come out and play*, they seemed to be saying.

With dogs, once I found them, I used treats to cajole them into the car. There was one time our dogs dragged a deer carcass (previously dead) up to our front yard, to the horror of my mom and sisters, but that was a one-time event.

Convincing horses to return often took all morning. Learned over millennia, their favorite game is allowing a human, holding a bridle and a rope, to get just within striking distance and then snort and trot off twenty yards, stop, and continue grazing. This went on for hours. I missed school several winter mornings playing this game.

I've seen the same kind of behavior (minus the deer carcass) in humans, especially kids. Once, in a Minnesota June, as a senior right before graduating from high school, I was in class finishing up a test. From under the room's dim, crackling fluorescent lights, we all looked longingly at the sun shining on fields of grass and corn outside. It was our last final.

Suddenly, one of the senior boys, with no warning, slid his chair over to the window, opened the window, jumped out, and ran.

Just like that.

Of course, he got in trouble, but not too much. It was our last week of school, and he was going right into the military. Yet I never forgot the lesson. Sometimes, after sitting for hours doing stuff that's not important to my life right now, it's the right decision to open a window, jump out, and run.

Our dogs understand: Life is short, the grass is green, the sun is shining, and the road goes over a hill and dives into a forest. Must go!

"Good Nellie, Good Girl"

This chapter is about changing behavior.

To start, one of my jobs is being a soccer coach. In Santa Fe, it seems everyone has multiple jobs. It's just that kind of culture — and maybe the future for a lot of us.

I started coaching soccer in 1998. Lots of kids, girls and boys, and lots of different ages, from six-year-olds (so much fun!) to seniors in high school. (With them, you must be on your toes; if they sense weakness, they'll kill and probably eat you — it's a tribal thing.)

The point is that coaching soccer and "coaching" dogs have a lot in common.

A little history: When I was in high school, I played American football. I loved football, but I was small and slow. From an inheritance of genes point of view, I think that was truly unfair.

I didn't play a lot, but I did nominate myself to be the captain of the left side of the bench. All the starters sat on the right side; the subs and hopefuls on the left. I won the imaginary vote in a landslide.

Our football coaches were ex-military. Football being football, practice was often brutal. We mumbled to ourselves that what they really were doing was preparing us to be drafted and sent to Vietnam. It was common for a coach to grab a player's face mask and throw the boy to the ground.

It was standard to make players run hills and sprints and do push-ups, not for fitness, but as punishment.

Best sport's movie of all time is *Remember the Titans* with Denzel Washington. In it, Coach Boone makes the team do "up-downs" because Blue is thirsty. ("Water is for cowards; water makes you weak. We're going to do up-downs until Blue is no longer tired and thirsty.")

To be fair, we loved it. We wanted to be tough, we wanted to play football. We would endure (and that's the right word) a lot to play. In my sophomore year, I shattered my jaw tackling a guy who was a foot taller and forty pounds heavier. When I finally got up from the ground, one of the coaches gave me salt water to gargle. I took a sip, and as I passed out from pain (it was an open fracture), I was thinking, *This is so cool!*

The point is, when I played football, the method for changing behavior on the football field was to punish, humiliate, criticize, and bench players.

In my first dog-training class (which as mentioned I flunked), the culture about changing dog behavior was the same. I had Shawnee in a metal choke collar. When she stepped out of line — barking, lunging, peeing — my task was to yank her down with the choke collar until she was on the floor and yell, "Bad dog!" If I found poop in the house, I was supposed to drag her by the collar, put her nose down by the offending object, and yell, "No! Bad dog!" When I did this, Shawnee just gave me a puzzled look, tail between her legs because she was afraid.

Like football practice, the goal seemed to be to catch a dog doing something "bad" and then punish them.

I think using punishment to change behavior is a cultural throwback to our puritanical ancestors who, among other things, put people in stockades and burned witches. Christianity also includes the meta-construct of "hell," the ultimate, forever burning, can't-pass-go punishment. Growing up Catholic, before I was ten, I memorized the mortal sins that could land you immediately in hell and many of the lesser, venial sins that could get you in trouble when you met St. Peter at the Pearly Gates.

The point is that our culture has long accepted punishment as the way to change behavior.

The problem is, this approach isn't very effective and can be counterproductive. Putting aside the fact that it is morally wrong to inflict pain on any being, the scientific results are "iffy."

First, punishment, while changing behavior in the short term, has all sorts of negative and unintended consequences. One example is the suppression of other behaviors, similar to the dogs in Martin Seligman's "learned helplessness" experiment (see pages 67–68). Chances are, those dogs avoided all sorts of other behaviors that had nothing to do with avoiding a shock. Since they weren't sure what might cause a shock, they became extremely, unnecessarily cautious and didn't do much at all. Next, both humans and dogs often exhibit a strong emotional response to being punished. When they are hurt, even in the name of changing a negative behavior, people and dogs can react with aggression.

Then there is the issue of intent. It is normal for humans to ascribe intention to any behavior. We pass someone in the hall and say hi, and if they don't reply, we instantaneously make assumptions — they don't like us, they're a jerk, or we're not worthy of respect (that's where I immediately go: *I'm a slug!*). Yet we really don't know their intentions. Maybe they didn't hear us, or maybe they were lost in their own problems. We don't know until we, um, ask.

It's the same thing with dogs. A dog pees on the rug. Are they disobeying us or being intentionally "bad"? We often assume so, but the reality might be that the dog was scared, or can't pee in the rain, or was simply left inside too long. It's vital not to assume bad intentions and punish what might have been an innocent mistake, an accident, or the result of our own actions. Remember, even with good intentions, we all still make mistakes.

With dogs, for punishment to effectively change behavior, the punishment must be delivered immediately, within a few seconds, and consistently — that means every time the dog poops on the rug, you must respond within seconds. That might work in a lab setting, but it's a silly, unrealistic expectation in everyday life.

Finally, we need to be aware of our own intentions. When we punish a negative behavior, are we genuinely trying to change that behavior, or are we punishing out of anger in order to make the dog (or anyone) feel bad? Punishing out of anger is abuse; the intention is to hurt. If we can't control our own emotions, the best advice is to detach ourselves from whatever the situation is and calm down before acting.

That is the Number One Rule for any adult.

If the goal is to change behavior, what is the most effective method?

Positive reinforcement.

This is the approach of metta, of loving-kindness toward all living and sentient creatures. Positive reinforcement is the way for a dog owner to stop their puppy from jumping up on their mother-in-law, and I break this down into two simple practices.

Ironically, it works the same with dogs and teenage soccer players.

First, always be on the lookout for when a dog (or a soccer player) is doing something right. Then, second, reinforce the hell out of it. We have been conditioned to see mistakes, the "oops." We need to train ourselves to see good behavior, when things are done the right way. When that happens, we can shower that dog or athlete with praise — or cookies. Cookies go a long way with soccer players....

Distraction is another useful, positive strategy. The moment a dog jumps up on a mother-in-law, distract the dog by engaging them in a game, a toy, or a treat. This is a better, more long-lasting method than yelling at the dog. Over time the puppy will associate the mother-in-law with something they like, increasing cooperation.

Here is the upshot. I never want a dog to be afraid of me because I've punished them. I don't want the experience, ever again, of nailing Shawnee to the floor in a choke collar with her tail between her legs. "Fear," Temple Grandin wrote, "is a very painful emotion for all animals and you don't want to base your relationship with an animal on fear."

What I want is for any dogs living with us to be happy to see me when I walk through the door. At night, when we sit on the couch, I wanted Nellie to come up to me and nestle her head on my lap so I could pet her and hug her and whisper, "Good Nellie, good girl."

Calm Human, Calm Dog

———————— ⌒⌒ ————————

Once on a fire department call, we responded to a multiple-car crash. Cars were all over the road and piled on top of one another. I got out of our medical unit, and I could feel myself getting "ramped up" because it looked like a critical incident. (There were no serious injuries, but we didn't know that at first.) People were running around screaming and yelling for help. The state police were arriving at high speed with their lights flashing and sirens screaming.

I was starting to breathe fast and get tunnel vision — when you get so upset that you see only what is in front of you. At just about that moment, a fire engine pulled up, a paramedic (more experienced than I) got out, looked over the scene, yawned, and said, "Well, let's get to work."

At that moment I said to myself, *No one is going to out-calm me!* I took a deep breath, worked on relaxing, and walked — not ran — over to the scene.

This call was a critical lesson for me in how to be effective as a firefighter when people all around you are panicked.

This has a direct lesson for us and our dogs. Temple Grandin wrote, "You are the grown-up and you need to stay calm if you want your dog to stay calm."

Dogs mirror our emotional states. If on a walk, we see another dog and human approaching, and we get nervous, our dog is going to sense that and go into protect mode. For example, say our dog gets loose and bounds down the street after another couple and their dogs. If we yell and scream at them to come back, the dog will probably think we're barking along with them: Something in the universe has gone terribly wrong and it has to do with these other dogs and humans. Our dog must do something about it! Okay, truth told, this happened to me. I did sprint after my dogs yelling at the top of my lungs. I'm sure that didn't help. They were probably thinking I was running to take on the humans while they handled the dogs.

As I chased them, I realized I was failing at staying calm. I worried that the fire department would find out and take away my "always calm" badge. Staying calm in the face of barking dogs or other adversity is an ongoing project: a day-to-day process and commitment. The first step is understanding that if we're calm, there is a better chance that our dog will stay calm. I even use a mantra in stressful situations (whether dog- or human-related). I repeat: "I will stay calm." It helps me focus on how I want to show up, stay focused, and solve the problem. The second step is physiological. We teach new firefighters how deep breathing can help them calm down. My favorite breathing technique (that I wish we could teach our dogs) is "square breathing." Breathe in four seconds, hold for four seconds, exhale for four seconds, and hold for four seconds, then repeat. It works! When I focus on my breathing, my shoulders drop, and I can feel myself relax.

The larger lesson is that if we can stay calm in a difficult world, we are more able to solve problems and deal with the insanity.

Be calm. Breathe. And maybe, just maybe, our dog will also.

Off-Leash in the Mountains

Of all the sights I love in this world — and there are plenty —
very near the top of the list is this one: dogs without leashes.

— Mary Oliver

And so it is with me.

Above Santa Fe, the Sangre de Cristo Mountains rise to over twelve thousand feet. There are three local peaks, Santa Fe Baldy, Lake Peak, and Penitente Peak. These are the southernmost peaks of the Rocky Mountains. My favorite is Penitente, which is another name for Los Hermanos, a Catholic order founded in the early nineteenth century. It began after the Mexican church withdrew its missionaries from the northern settlements in New Mexico and southern Colorado. The Penitentes stepped in as laymen to keep alive deep Catholic traditions in the small and isolated villages of *El Norte*.

There is a stone cairn atop Penitente. I have no idea who built it or when. Just a mystery in the mountains.

On one hike across the shoulder of Penitente, in the rocky scree, on what was just a trace of a trail, a fellow hiker reached down and pulled up a broken shard of blue-and-white pottery. It was ancient, Pueblo or Anasazi. It was another reminder of the centuries of occupation and travel through these mountains: history everywhere.

Mountains are best described as ridges and drainages. Millions of years of lifting, snow, water, blowing sand, and erosion create the drainages around Santa Fe, which ultimately flow into the Rio Grande and then to the Gulf of Mexico.

I write this because our Berners were, in theory, mountain dogs. They are named after the canton of Berne, Switzerland, where the breed was domesticated over thousands of years. Their history dates back to Roman mastiffs. The German name for the breed is *Berner Sennenhund. Sennen* means "to work in an alpine pasture" and *Hund* means "dog" in German.

They were bred to be farm dogs in the Swiss Alps, hauling carts and being barking companions for cattle. Ours never hauled carts and their cattle encounters were rare.

They did love the mountains above Santa Fe. As we drove up the winding road to the trailheads at the Santa Fe ski basin, the dogs would be whimpering with excitement in the car. As soon as we arrived and opened the doors, they jumped out, impatiently waited for us to get ready and put on their harnesses and leashes, and then we'd head up. As soon as we were out of the parking lot, on the trail, we took off the leashes and they were free!

Watching a dog off-leash in the mountains, heading up a drainage, is to see bliss. There is so much to smell, there are streams to drink from and lollygag in. There are other dogs also free and off-leash, dogs who up in the mountains know the "rules" of greeting and playing. And for our Berners, in spring and early summer, there was snow.

Snowdrifts left over from winter dotted the trails and slopes of the ski basin. Each one offered the opportunity to roll, slide, lay, lay upside down, and bury your paws and snout. Our walks up zigzagged from drift to drift and then to stream and mud. We humans trudged behind, smiles on our faces, watching.

Occasionally, we ran into a small herd of cattle grazing on the thick mountain grass. The Berner "cattle responsibility" was not to herd cattle, but mostly to hang out with them and defend them from predators. When our guys saw cattle, they were mystically drawn to them, and then one would bark in introduction. As all the heads of the cows raised up...the Berners did not know what to do next, so they headed back up the drainage.

Some hikers have a goal in mind, to climb a peak, to find the headwaters of a stream. Our goal was to meander, to be in the mountains, with no deadlines, no schedule, no phones, just be with our dogs in the aspens and ponderosas.

When I was alone with the dogs, when it was just Oso and I, or Tank and Nellie and I, there was this secret meadow, this special place tucked off a ski trail that we went to just to sit. It was strewn with massive boulders. Between the granite rocks were the flowers of the Rockies: blue columbine, red Indian paintbrush, yellow potentilla, and pink fireweed.

We collapsed and rested. I found a place to sit and the dogs, after a bit of checking out the meadow, lay down beside me. They even nodded off, as tired dogs are wont to do, and I sat there and listened to them breathe.

I could see across the Rio Grande rift. I could lay back and, in the summer, watch cumulonimbus clouds build into orographic thunderstorms. Ravens and crows shared the airspace and cackled from the trees. Bold gray jays, also known as camp robbers, hopped in close looking for scraps. They often landed on my outstretched hand and took treats.

The geographic question of my life — geography is destiny — is choosing between the mountains and the rolling hills and placid rivers of Minnesota.

The mountains seem frozen in time. Every morning you wake up and there they are, towering above. Yes, the light, the sun, the moon, the aspens in autumn, all these change the appearance of the mountains. In geologic time, they are moving, uplifting, and eroding at the same time.

But on a human scale, as it is written in Ecclesiastes, they abideth forever.

I choose the mountains. I choose to sit with the Rockies stretching north behind me, the state of New Mexico laid out at our feet, and content, free dogs choosing to stay by my side. I choose the mountains because they are wild, harsh, and dramatic in their beauty. I choose them because it is easier to be alone with dogs in mountain wilderness.

There was one time, with Nellie and Tank, when we stayed in our meadow until sundown. Then Nellie got up and stretched and looked at me expectantly. Stiff from the hike up, I slowly stood up and took her cue. Tank, always the last to rise, got up and we started down the trail.

Going down, the tired dogs stayed closer to me. Nellie still led the way, but constantly checked back to make sure we were going down. Tank trailed behind, head down, tramping just like any almost-to-the-end-of-day hiker.

As we approached the parking lot, I put their leashes

back on and there were no objections: better to be safe crossing the road. Getting to the car they both jumped in, settled down, heads on paws. They were wet, muddy, covered in mountain grit, and tired.

Our ride down was peaceful, no whining from the peanut gallery. But leaving the mountains conjures all sorts of feelings. From solitude to schedules. From the cool mountain air to the warmth of the high desert. From being with dogs to dealing with people.

As our dogs just want to be with us, and that is an evolutionary drive, I swear there are days I just want to be alone with them. In the mountains, ideally, but I am happy just being alone with them at home.

Growing up, at sixteen or so, one of my earliest girl friends (as in friend, not romantic) mentioned that when she thought of me, I was always with a dog. And I was. The most disconnected times of my life were when I was without a dog. I assigned dogs the role of best friend and canine consigliere. Although I abide humans, generally enjoy their individual company, and especially love my family, humans are *complicated*. If we actually listen to each other (let's face it, a rare thing), then we feel obligated to share our opinion, try to fix a problem, or just change the subject. Incomplete sentences, thoughts that just meander off into nothingness, admitting that things look hopeless and you have no idea what to do — these are greeted with raised eyebrows and judgment.

I know dogs can't understand most of the words I'm saying. Yet what human would stay by my side as I pace up and down the hallway asking aloud, for the hundredth time, why a girlfriend dumped me? Or why my sisters died? Or who would bump against my side as we walk down a mountain trail while I explained my relationship to the divine and why this mountain valley was my cathedral? Who?

Well, Tank did.

Sitting on a high trail with a dog next to me, both of us gazing into the middle distance, I feel open, that I can talk about anything. Nothing is out of bounds, big questions can be asked.

And when silence comes, when I am out of words, dogs don't feel like they must fill the void. They are comfortable resting their head on my lap and just being with me. The silence of dogs, laying quietly by my side. No agenda, no urgency to do something. Being there, absorbing my anxiety, glimmering a bit of light on my darkness. It is much easier to have those moments of silent clarity with a dog than it is with a human.

When we are done, when the sun arcs down, we walk toward civilization and family. We put away the excitement of the glittering stones and the ravens that circle us. Back and down. Back and down. Into a home of lovely people, of noise and food. Laurie asks, "Did you have a good time?" I always answer yes.

When an Old Dog Dies

Our EMT team once transported an elderly woman with a broken hip to the hospital. As we rolled her in on the gurney, a nurse clucked and said to me, "It's true for all of us. We're all TABs." I asked her what she meant, and she said, "Temporarily able bodies."

We all fall victim to the universe's rule: Stuff happens. Whether by accident, disease, or just wear and tear, our robustly healthy lives either abruptly end or taper off to the "last scene of all," as Shakespeare wrote, calling old age a "second childishness" and death "mere oblivion; sans teeth, sans eyes, sans taste, sans everything."

We are all TABs, and we each must deal with it in our own ways. (Even thirty-somethings!)

Of course, so do dogs. Nellie and Tank were in their ninth year when this became apparent. By big dog standards, they were old.

Allow me to sing the praises of old dogs. Old dogs are settled in their ways. They know the routine. As old dogs, Nellie and Tank met us in the morning at our bedside, just like they did ever since they were "velociraptors," and Nellie nudged me out of the bedroom toward the food bowls, just like every day since I could remember. Yet her "nudges" were much less aggressive. As a young dog, she engaged in a friendly battle, all three of us enthusiastic about the morning, to see who could get out the bedroom door first. Often, all of us got stuck in the doorway together like a scene from a slapstick comedy. In the hallway, Nellie barked and jumped up, nipping at my heels, happy to be up and awake.

As an older dog, Nellie was gentle — knowing that I'm not a morning person anymore, nor she a morning dog — but still insistent that we get going.

Tank, true to his colors as the follower, tagged behind, a whine in his voice, since he didn't like any shenanigans that might get in the way of being promptly fed.

Yet neither ate as voraciously as they once did. Nellie sometimes skipped meals altogether.

The rest of the day followed a well-worn path, with modifications. After breakfast, we walked. By his ninth year, Tank had trouble with his hind legs, so we left him behind. He barked valiantly, but I'm pretty sure that he was comfortable staying home.

Nellie still loved our walks, although she was then one-eyed (cancer took her left eye) and limped (due to three surgeries on her back legs).

She limped, I limped. TABs.

Our walks were calm. In the past, every dog, car, or individual caused an uproar of curiosity and leash pulling. Now, nothing really distracted. We were only concerned with loosening up old muscles after too much lying around.

In summer, the rest of their days were spent avoiding the heat and finding cool places to sleep. This required rotating positions as the sun climbed in the eastern sky and descended in the west, heating different areas of the house.

Tank arose with a groan when it got too hot, found the next cool spot, collapsed, and was deep asleep within minutes. Tank's daily routine allowed me to tell the time by just knowing where he was sleeping.

We stopped playing. We tried. I could get Nellie worked up to chase me, but it wasn't the same. The fierce desire to catch me as I ran around the kitchen island had been replaced by the comfort of knowing that I was an easy catch. She merely had to wait me out rather than run from one end of the house to the other. That was fine with me.

At night, after the dishes were done and we settled down in the living room, Nellie joined me on the couch, getting as close to me as she could, a 130-pound lapdog. There she fell asleep, snoring as was her right, as an old dog, to do.

Tank, depending on the heat and the presence of thunderstorms, curled up on the floor next to us, as he'd done every night throughout his life.

When it was late, and everyone else went to bed, Nellie inexplicably exited the dog door, preferring to sleep outside on the flagstone of the courtyard (part of a fenced-in yard). An old dog under the Milky Way and the night sky. Occasionally, late at night, we heard a deep-throated woof as she warned the coyotes that she was still here.

We grew old together. We wore down the same path, constant companions. We had great times in the mountains and had fun sliding in the snow.

The last summer Nellie and Tank were with us was hot. We all were looking forward to winter and cold temperatures. Yet I knew that our time together was finite. That made the "now" so much sweeter.

I've often wondered if dogs have a sense of their mortality. I certainly do — just seems to happen as you get older. One of the consequences is an emergent appreciation for each morning. Waking up, putting feet on the floor, and thinking, *Wow! I'm alive and well! I get to enjoy another day with family and our dogs.* All that other stuff (career, ambition) has just steadily faded from my attention.

In that last year with Nellie and Tank, it was as if the air had changed. We could feel their time here was coming to a close.

Did the dogs feel this? Was Nellie leaning into me just a bit harder? Was Tank just a wee bit less hardheaded?

I intuited an awareness, but in the end, there is the

impenetrable communication gap between dogs and us. I chose to believe that they were happy, that they knew they were part of our family and safe, taken care of and loved.

In December 2019, Tank's pain became intolerable. The vet came to our house, and Tank had his head on my lap as we put him to sleep. I cried. There could only be one Tank, and now he was gone.

Three months later, as the Covid pandemic raged, Nellie was diagnosed with a mass in her belly. She was in pain and basically immobile. We scheduled a time for the vet to come to our house to see what could be done.

That same night, Nellie went out to sleep on the flag-stones in the snow. When we found her the next morning, she had passed away: an old dog under the Milky Way and the night sky.

I was devastated. To this day, I still find myself cry-ing when I think about it. No chance to say goodbye, no opportunity to hold her one last time. We bundled her up in a blanket, carried her to our garage. Our wonderful vet, Dr. Amanda Mouradian, came to our house, and we lifted Nellie into the back of her truck. Away they went down our driveway — Nellie for the last time, not for a walk or for the escape to the mountains, but to be cremated.

The question comes to me: Why on earth does the death of a dog affect me so? As a firefighter and an old man, I am familiar with death in so many of her forms. Strang-ers have passed before me, family, friends, two of my sisters, and I've mourned, been shocked, been overwhelmed. You'd think that those deaths would allow a certain grace, a per-spective and a wisdom about death, that would ameliorate the intensity of what I feel. But no. The roaring is still there. The unanswerable question of why? In return, the implacable silence of the universe. The sinking sensation that no incantation or prayer can bring Nellie, or any dog or person, back.

So, no. I don't have an answer to my question. Rather I cling to what I've written before: *Our dogs die, and we must celebrate life.*

It is the way, the only way. Insanity ensues if we cannot bear our pain *and* dance a hora at a wedding. It is the hardest of things, yet it is the way. Don't talk to me about the phases of grieving or a timeline to "get over it." Grief, the writer Terry Tempest Williams wrote, is the raven on my shoulder. Each day as I awake, feet on the floor, glad to be alive, that raven sits there. We are close companions now. On those days when the raven spreads her wings, I choose to dance.

How to Be Old

Nellie was my "how to be old" teacher. No matter what happened to her, broken leg, torn ACL, weeks in a kennel at the vet's to limit her movement, blind in one eye, she just kept living.

Going to and from the veterinarian's clinic, she never growled or whined. She just accepted what was going on. When we had to leave her for days, she'd always wag her tail and try to jump up on me when we returned to get her.

Her spirit was stoic. She emanated grit, a determination that as long as she was with her people, she'd go on.

There are pleasures in being older. A deeper understanding of love. A better grasp of who is wise and who are fools. The importance of kindness. Of course, there is a better grasp of what is suffering versus what is inconvenience.

On the other hand, growing older has its downfalls. Standing in the grocery store, one you've shopped in for twenty years, wondering where the wine is, that's a big one. Soreness, aches, physical failures, and injuries are a daily topic of conversation with all my older friends. Banal (Covid and bronchitis) and exotic (tardive dyskinesia) diseases are something you become familiar with — and you drive your doctor daughter nuts with unending questions.

I remember sitting in a doctor's office. A man, older than I, was obviously perturbed. He was complaining to the poor receptionist, "What about the flatulence!" Laugh, but it's an important question. You find yourself on WebMD a lot searching for answers to those kinds of questions.

As you age, people question when you will stop driving. That question brings a conversation to an abrupt standstill. Every "older" person responds sharply with, "What! I've been driving since I was sixteen!" And then they furiously try to calculate how many years that has been. By then, the eyebrows have been raised and decisions by other people have been made. Other people making decisions for you is the bane of being "old."

All this goes on. Daily something new. Then when I looked at Nellie, curled by the fireplace, lying on a cool floor, blanket over her, and a daughter beside her. Perfect bliss.

What were Nellie's big lessons as we got older? First, love and allow yourself to be loved (no matter how weirdly some humans express their love). Next, learn to deliriously love each living day, season, starry night, warm wind in winter, cool breeze in summer, dinner with friends, grandchild, conversation with strangers (you can do that when you're old!), and eye roll of your children when you tell a terrible joke. Love each breath you take, and of course, the warm rough fur of a dog when you hug them.

Deliriously love those things.

Give up pretense. Nellie certainly did, walking around with one eye sewed shut. No one cares. You can wear cargo shorts and Birkenstocks if you wish and top it off with a T-shirt that reads *"El Viejo"* and a Minnesota Twins baseball hat.

Walk often. Nap daily. Do work you love until the day you die. (In the Bhagavad Gita, it's written, "If I did not work, these worlds would perish.") Nellie never stopped barking to warn us about coyotes or delivery drivers.

Next, and I do not know if Nellie could do this, accept that you will die. Accept it, get over it, it's okay to be afraid, it's okay to wish for no pain. Most importantly (think 72-point type here), let the people you love know you love them. Family and friends. The word love is not diminished by its use. Use it a lot.

Finally, if you can, choose to pass outside under a starry sky. I think that is why Nellie chose to sleep outside that final night. To that I say yes. Give me that.

The poet Dalia Shevin has her own vision, which she describes in the poem "In My Good Death":

I will find myself waist deep in high summer grass. The humming
shock of the golden light. And I will hear them before I see
them and know right away who is bounding across the field to meet
me. All my good dogs will come then, their wet noses
bumping against my palms, their hot panting, their rough faithful
tongues. Their eyes young and shiny again. The wiry scruff of
their fur, the unspeakable softness of their bellies, their velvet ears
against my cheeks. I will bend to them, my face covered with
their kisses, my hands full of them. In the grass I will let them knock
me down.

Part 5

Wait ... We Have a Chihuahua?

*Dogs die. But dogs live, too. Right up until they die,
they live. They live brave, beautiful lives. They protect their
families. And love us. And make our lives a little brighter.
And they don't waste time being afraid of tomorrow.*

— Dan Gemeinhart, *The Honest Truth*

My daughters can be annoying. They are highly opinionated, political, and dog loving.

A few years ago, when they both reached that age where everything their parents did or said was suspect, they accused me of being "sizeist," of only liking big dogs. After some hemming and hawing, I pled guilty. I've been surrounded by big dogs since I was ten: German shepherds, collies, and Bernese mountain dogs. Small dogs were never on my, or Laurie's, radar. Most of this was ignorance, with a little fear tossed in. Big dogs seem strong, powerful, and able to take care of themselves. The vision of our shepherd, Shawnee, leaping a fence onto an aggressive horse or pushing little kids away from a pool has stuck with me as what a dog should be. A small dog seemed vulnerable, easy to get lost or attacked. As bad, I might accidentally step on a small dog and hurt it.

Admittedly, I had blinders on and a little rigidity in my thinking. Daughters are great at poking at that, uncomfortable as it might be.

Daughters being daughters, they also hammered home that there was need in the shelters. Sully, our youngest, dragged me to volunteer at the animal shelter in Santa Fe. Brynne, in her spare time away from school, began regularly sending pictures of cute, and small, shelter dogs.

As is a well-known fact in familyhood, when the women decide, they can bend steel with their minds. First, Laurie opened to the idea of a small dog. Her argument was that we were not getting any younger and as "older people," we couldn't have a 130-pound dog jumping up on us. That sealed the deal. It looked like a small dog was in our future. But how it happened, well, remember that old saying about how, when we make plans, the gods laugh?

No Little Dog Is Going to Win My Heart ...

Here is how it happened. As children do, our daughter Brynne had grown up, moved out, gone to school on the East Coast, come back to town, and was living with her boyfriend and working at a local bar before starting medical school. Luke (the boyfriend and later husband) had a roommate. That roommate had acquired a shih tzu mix from a puppy mill. Tallulah was from an "unintentional" litter and was looking at a precarious future. She was a tiny, tiny puppy.

As anyone could have predicted, knowing our family's obsession with dogs, Brynne fell head over heels for Tallulah, and with Luke's assistance, they slowly took over her care and feeding. Finally, the roommate admitted that he was out of his league, and Tallulah became Brynne's next canine love affair.

When I first met Tallulah, I could hold her comfortably in one hand. She was so little and fragile. I was used to puppies like our Berner Tank, who as a puppy could run full speed into a wall and then just want to eat.

This was an entirely different type of dog. Vacuum cleaners were actually a threat. She could get lost under any piece of furniture. She could get stepped on. And there was no way she could go outside alone!

Anyway, this was what was going on in my head when Brynne insisted that I hold her.

Damn. She looked up at me, those brown eyes, that psychic message *I trust you* was passed, and I melted an infinitesimal amount. As in, I got how someone could love this little package, but no way could *I* take care of her. I'd be way too anxious.

But I was cool. After all, it was Brynne's puppy, not mine, right? I could go home, and life would go on.

And then…

"Dad," Brynne opined one day, "I'm bringing Tallulah over for the weekend. You are going to dog-sit."

She paused and then said the words that always make me nervous, "It will be good for you!"

Fathers of daughters, join me in explaining to the world how terrifying those words are when they come from a woman you've raised — when they turn the tables and begin giving you advice, lasering in on the weaknesses in your character.

This is my journal of my first weekend with a dog so small she could sleep in my backpack:

Friday, 9:47 p.m.: Tallulah arrived. She was a little ball of white fluff, with dark eyes. I steeled myself, not wanting to get drawn in. She rolled over on her back, clearly confident that I was an easy mark.

Brynne looked at me, "See, Dad! She likes you!"

I could only think, *She's so small!*

11 p.m.: Brynne departed.

After a few minutes of clawing at the door and tiny whining, Tallulah walked back into our kitchen. A word about her "clawing." Over the years, our big dogs have nearly clawed through doors. Tallulah's attempts at scratching were a relief.

Saturday, 1 p.m.: I began to worry Tallulah might be lonely. I sat down on the floor and watched her play with our dog toys, all of which were bigger than she. As Tallulah disappeared underneath a stuffed rabbit, Tank and Nellie watched with disgust. I'm sure they were thinking, *What is the point of having toys you can't destroy as soon as the humans bring them home?*

4 p.m.: All the dogs fell asleep.

Our big guys were splayed across the floor. Tallulah had strategically found a place underneath a stool to sleep. You never know when clumsy humans or slightly jealous Berners might step on you. Hmmm, I thought — smart move.

5:30 p.m.: After it rained, we took all three dogs for a walk.

Our dogs galumphed along looking for rabbits. I found myself suddenly scanning the sky looking for hawks. It had just occurred to me that Tallulah was the perfect hawk-size treat. I decided to stay very close, which was hard because Tallulah spent the entire mile zooming back and forth (on a leash; I had three dogs on leashes). Although we only went a mile, in Tallulah land, it was a marathon of running! Amazingly high rpm! Four running steps to the Berners' one.

7 p.m.: All dogs conked out.

8:30 p.m.: My "lapdog" jumped up on the couch — 130 pounds of snoring upside-down Berner, head on my lap. Tallulah jumped up and sat on the last foot of the couch, looking at me. Kinda cute, I thought. I again caught myself, *Do not get sucked in!*

Then Tank began his maniacal barking, indicating the Imaginary Intruder was back. All three dogs began barking at the wall. Pretty funny, two huge Berners and one tiny white ball of fur. *Woof! Woof!* And, *Yip! Yip!*

11 p.m.: Tallulah curled up on the bed with Sully, daughter number two. I wondered, *Why doesn't she sleep on our bed?* I suppressed that thought.

Sunday, 10 a.m.: I took Tallulah outside on a tiny patch of actual grass. She immediately began rolling around. Our big dogs crashed through fields in the mountains, only their tails visible as they flushed birds, rabbits, and the occasional coyote. Meanwhile, Tallulah lay in our yard exploring grass: the stems, tillers, and vertical lines on the blades. The small dog's world.

4 p.m.: I ran out to go on a fire department assignment.

When I came back, Tallulah was gone! Brynne had picked her up. Not a goodbye! Not a "See you soon"! I felt a little hurt.

9 p.m.: I couldn't stand it. I threw on a pair of jeans and an old white T-shirt. I drove across town to Brynne's house.

I got out of the car and started yelling, "Tallulah!!!!!!"

Okay, this last scene is from *A Streetcar Named Desire*. But that's how I felt.

Rescuing Maisie

My daughter Brynne is one of those people that animals *find*. First there was Tallulah. Then Brynne and Luke adopted a cat, Clover, who had been found nearly dead in an arroyo.

Next is Maisie's story. One afternoon when Brynne came home from medical school in Albuquerque, there was this little white dog wandering the street by her house. No collar, no tags. Scared and shaking.

Brynne coaxed the dog into her home, put one of Tallulah's coats on her, and gave her food and water.

She put up signs around the neighborhood that afternoon.

That evening a young woman knocked on their door. She told Brynne that the puppy (she said she was less than a year old) had gotten out of the garage while she was at work. She thanked Brynne and took the little one back home. End of story. Everyone relieved. And then...

A few days passed.

The woman came back to Brynne's home, the dog in tow on a leash.

"I got Maisie on an impulse at a flea market," the woman said. "But that was a big mistake. I just can't handle a dog right now. I'm going to take her to a shelter unless you want her."

Maisie was a mess. She was dirty, thin, and scared.

Brynne thought, *Shelter or my house?* She did the calculus in her head, consulted Luke, and then said, "We'll take her."

The woman thanked her again, handed Brynne the leash, and left.

Just like that.

So now Brynne had two little dogs and a recovering cat. This was a lot for a medical student and a working fiancé.

What do you do when you feel in over your head?

You call your mom.

I was unaware of the initial machinations between the two of them. Like many dads, I was in my own world of playing with the Berners, playing a lot of soccer, and occasionally working — happy oblivion. A few days later I was drawn into the conversation.

There was no way that Brynne was going to take this little pup to a shelter, but having three animals to take care of was just too much. The obvious solution: Laurie and I would take Maisie.

Laurie and I talked for about thirty minutes. I had been softened by Tallulah to the small-dog experience, but how would Maisie get along with our big but old guys? Should we keep her in the house and not let her tempt the hawks and coyotes? We both knew we'd say yes, but we wanted to make sure we were ready for a third dog.

Sully was adamant that we take her, so the vote was unanimous.

A few days later, Brynne and Luke showed up with their menagerie: Tallulah, the family "head" dog; Clover-the-cat, who now lived to intimidate everyone; and this thin and scared puppy, Maisie.

They spent the night and we let Maisie get used to us and the big dogs. It didn't take long for her to play with Tank, and Nellie grudgingly accepted her.

Brynne and Luke left on a Sunday afternoon. Maisie, like Tallulah, whined and scratched at the door when they left, then just sat there.

From a puppy mill to a cage in a flea market to a woman who did not want her to wandering the streets to another family and then to us. And so began the long process of bonding with a dog who probably believed that, as J.D. Salinger wrote, life was hell.

It usually takes months for a rescue to adjust to a new home. They're nervous, prone to escape, and cautious around humans. Fortunately, Tank and Nellie were there, so Maisie had dogs to bond with and from whom she could learn the ropes. (Like the dog door!)

In the beginning, she growled when we tried to pick her up. She slept by herself and was picky about food. She spent a lot of time shaking.

We just kept telling ourselves that it would take time.

We learned that rescues, like highly anxious people, need a routine they can depend on. A morning meal. Morning walks with treats. Naps and alone time. A bit of play with the other dogs. Another nap. Maybe a second walk or some time outside. Dinner, then sleep. Repeat.

As her fear melted away, she became friendly and assertive. She started to bark at anyone and everyone on our walks. This was not a big deal because she was all of twelve pounds. But it made me wonder...

We weren't sure what Maisie was. She looked like a terrier, or a Westie (West Highland white terrier), or a combination of every small breed. We decided to do a DNA test.

As we waited for the results, and I worried that I was right, lots of opinions were shared and wagers made.

The results: Maisie was 50 percent, you guessed it, Chihuahua. The rest of the mixes didn't matter; we had adopted and began to love a *Chihuahua*.

A note: As a firefighter, the only dog that ever went for my throat on a call was a Chihuahua that we rescued, I repeat, *we rescued*, from a car crash. Okay, that Chihuahua, whose name was Angel, was no doubt terrified, but hey, we were the good guys!

That encounter colored my opinion of Chihuahuas.

Masie was not only part Chihuahua, but she was a New Mexican part Chihuahua. Around here, Chihuahuas are an art form; they are an iconic part of the dog landscape. They're loyal, irascible, and so are their guardians. You see them in funny hats (the dogs, not the guardians), in backpacks in line at the grocery store, where they glare at you, and being held by their people under one arm while they shop.

I was reputationally torn. On the one hand, I was beginning to enjoy Maisie and all her quirks. On the other hand, that male voice kicked in: *I can't be seen walking a Chihuahua!*

I tried to explain my dilemma to the women in my life. I received multiple lectures on toxic masculinity, on growing up, on just being myself. That last one meant that everyone could see that I loved playing with Maisie, and I shouldn't be shy about walking her in public. As in, get over it.

I had to manage my "self-talk." I reminded myself that Maisie might be little, yet she had the heart of a much larger dog. She was fearless (a little too fearless at times), and she loved walking.

You know those moments when you are well and truly busted? Where you run right into all the preconceived notions that you carry and discover they are made up, wrong, and sorta crazy? Maisie disabused me of an entire set of prejudices I was holding about Chihuahuas. I hate when that happens, but it did, and I am wiser for it.

Except for one thing. Because she is small, I am over-the-top protective of her. I need to know where she is, that all the doors are locked, and the dog door secured so that she can't be outside alone when we're gone or at night. When she is in our courtyard, alone, lying in the sun, I reorient my desk and chair so that I can keep an eye on her. The last thing I do at the end of the day is check out where she sleeps, just because. Finally, when Maisie and I do solo walks, I am hypervigilant about coyotes, hawks, and other dogs.

Truth be told, I became the typical proud guardian of a half-Chihuahua: protective, irascible, and defensive. There are no funny hats and no carrying her in a backpack (yet). But she is the first dog we've ever had that has traveled with us on planes. Flight attendants love her. This caught my attention from a purely academic perspective. As a researcher of all things canine — and this seems important — women seem unusually interested in men who have small dogs. It's a mystery and let's just leave it at that. Nothing could be gained from me elaborating on this point.

Although it took time — and who can blame her — Maisie settled in to being "our dog." I knew there had been a sea change in her when one night she climbed the "dog stairs" to our bed, found the bend in my knees, curled up there, nose to tail, and went to sleep. A dog's way of saying I trust and love you. I remember putting my hand on her head and relaxing: We were her guardians.

Get Down on Your Belly
and Investigate the Tall Grass

As I've mentioned, umwelt is the idea that our perception creates our reality. A great example of this is the world of the small dog. The road Maisie and I take on our walks is asphalt, and it cuts through high desert grasses, piñon, juniper, a few ponderosas, and in a wet summer, lots of wildflowers. Maisie wanders back and forth on the walks, into the grasses, and then when she moves a little quicker (her choice, I'm perfectly happy meandering), she gets back on the road.

One walk, on a whim one day, I lay down on my belly next to the tall grass to see what Maisie sees. It was eye-opening. The grass along the road (two to three feet tall) towered over my head. I couldn't see what was beyond it. Since I don't have Maisie's ability to smell, I had no idea what was lurking there. I then better understood why she doesn't go leaping into the grass. Rather, she always smells around a bit and then slowly moves into what must seem like a forest to her. Intrigued, I did the same thing at home. I lay down on our living room floor and noticed how "big" everything seems. When my daughter Sully walked in, she looked like a giant. (She did suspiciously ask me what I was doing.)

Maisie navigates a world wholly different than ours. This is why Tallulah, Brynne's shih tzu mix, slept under tables or perched on the shoulders and backs of couches. Small dogs must be alert for all that goes on lest they be stepped on.

The bigger lesson is, of course, about empathy: the ability to see and share the perspective of others; to understand the world, if only temporarily, through their senses; to experience someone else's umwelt. In doing so, we better understand why others do the things they do.

I highly recommend that all small-dog guardians lie down and see anew their dog's world.

The larger lesson of umwelt is that we each have widely different experiences of reality. Letting go of our experience of reality as "truth" is vital in order to be compassionate and caring individuals.

My perspective while standing on the road, looking out at the horizon of grasses, is only one possibility, only one "reality." Maisie's is completely different — as is every person's, every sentient being's. Empathy makes the world a much richer place. Once we open up to different experiences, different ways of perceiving, we are in for an astonishing journey.

I have a small dog to thank for reminding me of that.

We Lied about Never Getting Another Big Dog

I was launched into the air. I flew by Laurie, horizontally, being towed by a super strong Great Pyrenees who was sprinting toward another dog on the road. I landed hard and, as I recall, bounced. Groaning, I said to Laurie, "We need to train this dog!"

After Nellie and Tank passed, Laurie and I agreed that big and rambunctious dogs were probably not a good idea for us anymore, since we were "older." (Not old, just older. Huge difference.) Yet apparently, neither one of us truly believed that we weren't still thirty years old.

It was spring 2020. Our two Berners had passed away and our house was quiet. No raucous barking when a delivery truck showed up, just Maisie's annoyed little bark at being jarred awake from a midday nap. Maisie was not a watch dog or a guard dog. She was just a dog who was easily *irritated*.

We were in lockdown due to the pandemic, so both Laurie and I were home a lot, and we were grieving the loss of Nellie and Tank. Our daughter Brynne had moved to Minnesota for work, and she worried about our current state of dogs. Our daughter Sully kept leaving hints that all was not right in our household.

Thus, in May, all of us independently were looking at dogs on the Santa Fe Humane Society website.

Serendipity happens.

This big white dog with a black-and-white face — it was hard to tell what breed, not that it mattered — caught our attention, all of us on the same day.

Time for a family council. It was clear that the votes were leaning toward "this is the dog," but we knew nothing about him.

Maybe it was the pandemic, how it twisted our sense of reason, logic, and time. Maybe it was because we missed Big Dog spirit. In any case, Laurie and I mutually "forgot" her warning that we were too old for a big dog.

I called the shelter. The dog was a Great Pyrenees mix. His name was Toby. The shelter estimated that he was a year or so old. He weighed in at eighty pounds, so not a huge dog — that was our rationalization. The excitement built as I shared this information with the family. Then came the crushing news: He'd already been adopted, and there was a waiting list for him if the first adoption did not work out.

But the experience taught us that we wanted another dog.

A couple of weeks passed as we continued our search.

Then out of the blue, we got a call from the shelter saying that Toby was available. I asked what had happened. The story we got was disquieting. The first family had returned Toby because he was simply too much to handle. A second family adopted him, but when they put him in a crate while they were gone, he got out and destroyed some furniture and a door trying to escape. So that couple returned him to the shelter.

The woman on the phone had a fatalistic tone, as if to

say she completely understood if this story made us change our minds.

I said I'd call her right back. I guess you could say that, for better and often for worse, we are an optimistic family. Our motto is "What could possibly go wrong?"

We discussed. We looked at the video again. We did some quick research on Great Pyrenees, glossing over a lot of facts. They bark. They tend to be not super obedient. They "come" when they bloody well want to. They are more stoic than Bernese mountain dogs. They were bred to be alone with sheep in the Pyrenees protecting the herd from wolves. Then we recalled other dogs who had damaged our homes. That brought a pause. But optimists always, we vowed never to crate Toby. We figured someone would almost always be home, and Maisie would be there to keep Toby company. We voted again. It was a unanimous yes. I called the shelter back and we set the adoption in motion.

No one knew anything about Toby's first year. After he was dropped off at the shelter, he was there a month before being adopted and rejected twice.

On our way to meet Toby, we wondered out loud about what that might do to a dog. Like Maisie, does being passed around, no permanent home, make a dog insecure, frightened?

We were about to find out.

The first step was meeting him. When we arrived, he was alone in a big outdoor pen at the shelter. After I slipped into the pen, he ignored me. Then, because I had treats, he eventually came over to check me out. He jumped back every time I tried to pet him, so I just sat down and let him be. This was not a dog, like many at the shelter, who craved human companionship.

Once he got used to me, it was Laurie's turn. He was much more responsive to Laurie. I took note. I was slightly jealous. Finally, the next big test was to see if he got along with Maisie. We took him back into the shelter, into a small room, where we carefully introduced the two. We all held our breaths, kept Maisie on a taut leash, and...nothing. They sniffed each other and that was that.

Success!

We did the paperwork and took Toby and Maisie out to the car. He jumped right in and never looked back. We were the new guardians of what would turn out to be an amazing dog. We vowed that, hell or high water, we'd be his new forever family.

There would be a lot of high water....

Watching a dog come into a new home is fascinating. They all have different approaches. When Maisie first came in, she looked around and sat on Sully's lap and just shook. She was scared — of the house, the people, the big dogs. Everything seemed strange.

Toby got out of the car, went right inside, did a perimeter check of every room, immediately found the dog door, went outside, did another perimeter check of the fenced yard, and then lay down outside, ignoring us. Toby seemed to want to be left alone.

Our first walks, except for me flying down our driveway, were uneventful. Toby kept his head down, following scent trails along the road. In the house, within days, he found a chair that he liked. It was in the center of the house and up against a window that faced the front yard. This way he could keep watch over what we presumed he considered his new territory. He had yet to decide whether we were his new "herd."

A few weeks went by. He escaped once and lit out for the territory, but he wandered back by himself. We took that as a good sign; maybe he was seeing us as family and home.

He slept on our couch at night, didn't bark a lot, played with Maisie, and never growled or was the slightest bit aggressive. All in all, he seemed to be relaxing into "our dog." I figured new dogs took six months to settle into their true nature, but Toby was a fast learner.

Always the optimists, ones who don't obsessively anticipate every possible scenario, that summer Laurie and I decided to pack up our house and drive to Minnesota. Brynne was expecting her second child in a few weeks, and we wanted to support her and Luke and spend time with our first grandkid, Fiona. Sully decided to join us, so that made our group a half Chihuahua, a Great Pyrenees that was just getting to know us, and three humans hauling a trailer during the pandemic.

Like I said, what could possibly go wrong?

When a Dire Wolf Runs
Across a Golf Course

The drive from Santa Fe to Minnesota during that first summer of the Covid pandemic was like *The Grapes of Wrath* redux. The atmosphere was stressed, with whiffs of panic because no one knew what the future held. The roads and interstates were packed with families on the move, in masks, staying away from "others" at gas stations and hotels. Pandemic politics were on full display. "Mask up" in some places (Santa Fe, the Denver part of Colorado, Minnesota), while others were defiantly "no mask" (eastern Colorado, Nebraska, Iowa). The American divide was hardening.

We chugged along in our little bubble of family, dogs, cleaning supplies, and a trailer packed with furniture, plants, and stuffed animals.

Our plan was to stay in Minnesota for the summer, hunker down, and wait out Covid with all of us, and a new baby, together. During that time, all Laurie and I wanted was for all of us to be together, family, dogs, and Clover-the-cat.

Things went awry.

On the Fourth of July, after we'd been in Minnesota for a few weeks, Toby and I were walking in a neighborhood close to our daughter's house. It was clearly a patriotic neighborhood; flags were everywhere. Flags on flagpoles and those little metal flags that you stick in the ground at the end of your driveway.

Up to then, everything had been going well with Toby. The drive up to Minneapolis, dog-wise, had been uneventful. The transition to Brynne's house, except for Maisie and Toby chasing each other through the house, had been acceptable.

Toby was coming into his own. Keeping on our normal schedule, we walked every morning. He greeted other dogs with a big *woof!*, but other than that, he was turning out to be (we thought) a chill dog.

This walk was a turning point. It was like watching an always friendly and loving child hit puberty and turn into a teenager — I've already worn out the velociraptor analogy, but you get my drift.

Down this neighborhood street we meandered. I wasn't paying much attention until I felt a tug on the leash. I looked behind and Toby had his leg up and was peeing on one of those metal *American* flags. *On the Fourth of July.* Not a marking kind of pee, but a full-on, bladder-bursting, thirty-second pee.

My first reaction was to glance around and see if anyone was looking. Nope, but thirty seconds are forever when you are mortally embarrassed. I didn't know whether to just run for it or go to the door of the house in question, apologize, and offer to hose off the flag.

Duh. I decided to run. At that moment, a woman and a poodle came out of the house across the street, and Toby chose this time, of all times, to hellaciously bark. I had a metal flag dripping with pee and a dog determined to wake up the entire neighborhood.

I pulled on his leash, waved to the poodle woman to distract her, and pleaded for Toby to hush.

It took about a block of jogging before he stopped barking and I figured we were out of danger. By danger, I mean being lectured about letting my dog disrespect the flag on July Fourth, of all days!

That day, that moment, Toby showed his true colors. He was going his own way. He was going to bark at anything that seemed out of place. At Brynne and Luke's house, Toby was set off by every delivery, and during the pandemic, there were lots. Toby ran around the house barking, making sure everyone was awake. His bark ranged from a normal *woof* to a howl and even a bit of a screech. At this point we renamed him Toby Thunderbark. It seemed appropriate.

However, Brynne's baby was due soon. Their modus operandi was to keep the house as Zen-like as possible. We knew this, yet we ignored the ramifications of introducing two new dogs into a peaceful household.

Our normal existence of chaos — barking, unfinished sentences, chasing Toby through the house, wrestling dogs away from the front door — was just not acceptable.

The unspoken arrangement was that Laurie was there to help with Fiona and help Brynne, while I was responsible for the canines. Toby was becoming an "issue."

Then one lovely summer morning, still waiting for the baby to arrive, we decided to take everyone to the zoo and leave the three dogs — Tallulah, Maisie, and Toby — at home with Clover-the-cat. We figured it would only be a few hours. I had a twitch of anxiety because we had never left Toby without humans, and he was going through this defiant teenager stage. But I didn't listen to that as our family motto popped into my head: *What could possibly....*

We were at the zoo for less than thirty minutes when Laurie's phone rang. A woman said, "Hey, we have your dog."

Bravo for dog tags! But holy cow, we had a dog on the loose in a strange town.

After a moment of silence, without any discussion, Laurie and I turned and headed for our car.

On our fast and furious drive back, it dawned on us that if Toby had gotten out, it was possible that the other dogs (small and vulnerable) and Clover-the-cat (rarely allowed outside) might also have gotten loose.

If something happened to them...well, that would be bad!

We slammed into the driveway to find both the little dogs outside. They were seriously happy to see us. Fortunately, Clover, being a cat, had ignored everything canine and was sleeping upstairs.

We turned into detectives. First, we noted that there was a big dog-size hole in the screen on the screened-in porch. Looking further, we noted that the house door leading to the porch was open, and there were huge scratches on the door.

I called the woman who had Toby, and she told me that he was happily playing with their two Labs in a pond, and she gave me directions. As the dog runs, their house was about two miles away. Toby had crossed two swamps, a road, and a busy golf course to get there. He runs like a wolf, and from a distance he looks like Ghost, the dire wolf from *Game of Thrones*. I'm sure that got some attention. It may have cost an unsuspecting golfer a few strokes.

I arrived at the house. I called Toby, and unbelievably, he came right to me, jumped in the car, completely soaked, and lay down without even looking at me. I thanked the family, and we headed back to what I knew was going to be an inquisition.

And it was.

By the time we arrived home, Toby was asleep, but the die had been cast.

In retrospect, this was a "high water" moment for Toby. But no one even wondered about giving him up. He was our dog and we were committed to keeping him.

We huddled and talked about next steps. It was clear that Laurie and Sully needed to stay in Minnesota to help Brynne, Luke, Fiona, and the new baby. Sensing this, I said that the best thing to do was for me to drive home with Toby (Laurie and Sully could fly home later).

It took a couple of days to make a plan, and then Toby and I hit the road and headed southwest. It was a male bonding trip. We talked, played music, and stayed in a cheap motel in Ogallala, Nebraska. In Colorado, we hit a dog park and ran around for an hour. Eight hours later we were home. Toby went in, reconnoitered, and then jumped up on the couch.

The next few weeks were just Toby and me. And although I missed the family, spending some alone time with our still-new dog was the right thing to do.

Here's the thing. I thought Toby was doing well. He was a loyal, strong, year-and-a-half-old puppy. He was next in a long line of not-so-perfect dogs. Maybe he wasn't designed to travel, maybe he was more comfortable being at home.

Home: I think that is the north star for a dog like Toby. After an uncertain puppyhood, living at the shelter, being rejected twice, maybe a home, that familiar place, was what he wanted most.

For a dog, "home" smells the same. Toby knows the location of his food and water bowls; he can find them in the dark. Outside, he knows where the coyotes run. The couch where he sleeps has an imprint from his body. He knows what time to come to our bedroom in the morning to get us up.

This is what home means. A place you'll never be taken from. A place that is yours.

There are wanderlusts and homebodies. My father was a wanderlust. He had a bag packed and ready to go, and he was as comfortable in Delta Air Lines seat 11C as he was sitting in his office. (Later, because he was a multi-million-mile passenger, he opted for 1B.)

Much has been written about wanderlusts, the adventurers. Steve McQueen famously said that he'd rather wake up in the middle of nowhere than any place else on earth. I was mesmerized by the story of Sir Ernest Shackleton and his crew forgoing home and sailing to Antarctica only to be trapped there for nearly two years. I have friends who climb in Nepal, others who on a moment's notice will pack their car and head farther west to California and the ocean. Wanderlusts.

In every life, there is a season for that.

And there is a season for home.

Toby seems to channel my mom. She was a homebody. For decades I traveled a lot for work. Now, as when I was under my mom's spell, I am again happy to hang out with Toby and Maisie and watch the daily change in the sky and in our garden.

On our drive to New Mexico, Toby and I relaxed a little more with every mile closer to home. After we arrived, Toby fell into his routines. We walked the same road daily. He patrolled the yard, slept on the couch, rested by me as I worked, and watched me out the window as I gardened.

I've never seen him restless or seemingly bored (how can you tell with a dog?). He was content. I thought about that a lot.

Much of it goes back to what we absorb from our early families. My dad came home from a trip excited with big ideas. He brought pictures of all the amazing and exotic places he had visited. Once, in a cold Minnesota February, he took my sister Patty on a business trip to Carmel-by-the-Sea, California. They stepped off the plane and drove to the hotel. They arrived with Minnesota translucent winter skin into seventy-degree weather and the smell of the ocean. My sister turned and punched him in the shoulder, saying, "This place exists, and we live in Eden Prairie, Minnesota?"

He just sheepishly shrugged his shoulders.

His travels took my breath away.

My mom, on the other hand, would ask me to walk through her garden. In the summer, there were lilacs and geraniums. We watched black ants climb into the peony blossoms. She told me the names of trees and why she loved dandelions. She threw sticks to our dogs, and they tagged along.

My dad's world seemed so big, and my mom's so small. I was always torn between the two.

It took me decades to learn, with a little help from Toby, that there is a season for both.

My season then and now is to be home, to write, to tend our garden, and walk our dogs. Occasionally, there is an amazing thunderstorm or a blizzard that would make my mom happy. My dream is, like her, to stand by a window, drinking coffee with two dogs by my side, and watch a storm turn the world white.

Like Toby, home means something special to me. Roots, comfort, safety. A place to explore. A place to watch the seasons change. I don't hold the genes of Shackleton's crew or my Nepal climbing friends.

Laurie, Sully, and Maisie came home in August. Toby and I were excited to see them. The house buzzed with a little more activity, the Cooking Channel always on and regular FaceTime calls with Brynne and her family. Seeing Fiona and my new grandson, Dash, was a mandatory evening activity. (We made plans to go back to Minnesota for Thanksgiving and let the dogs stay with a dog sitter.)

My secret dream was that we could all live together, kids, grandkids, dogs, and one cat. Maybe not under one roof, but close enough so that Fiona and Dash, when they were older, could walk to our house to sit and do homework at our kitchen table. Brynne and Luke had an old horse barn on their property, and I mused about converting it to a house for Laurie, Sully, and me. That idea was shot down: Brynne and Luke made it clear that they didn't want us *that* close. (Maybe I'll just keep mentioning the idea. I might wear them down....)

The pull of family and grandchildren is strong. For now, we live apart, some of us in New Mexico, some in Minnesota, and we typically drive through Nebraska and Iowa to see each other. Maybe with a few more years under his belt, Toby will calm down and we'll make the trip with him again. Maybe this time he'll be able to stay.

Resilience

A working definition of resilience from the American Psychiatric Association is "the process of adapting well in the face of adversity or trauma, the ability to bounce back after difficulty."

Before we adopted Maisie and Toby, we were of the view that the first few months of a dog's life set in stone the behavioral characteristics they would hold for the rest of their lives. Whether they liked being with children, were scared, friendly, or aggressive, these traits were set during the first few months of life.

Based on that belief, we avoided older shelter dogs and opted for puppies so that we could control those critical few months.

Of course, like human children, the early phase of a dog's life is crucial for the development of character.

And it is not the full story.

Maisie and Toby are anecdotal proof of that. They both came from questionable backgrounds. Maisie was a street dog, thin and scared of everything when we adopted her. Toby's puppy history is unknown, but he bounced from shelter to family and back to shelter before he came to live with us.

Both dogs have become tail-wagging, friendly, loyal, and easy to be with. My only caveat is that Maisie has her moments of aggression. I think it's her Chihuahua blood, but the argument has been made that, more likely, it is because she's a small dog who is still contending with a difficult upbringing. She exhibits submissive behavior often, rolling over on her back or backing away when we approach too quickly. We've learned that we must let her come to us rather than go to her.

They are not perfect dogs. I have only met a couple of "perfect" dogs, my daughter Brynne's shih tzu mix, Tallulah (she paid me to write that), and our neighbor's golden retriever, Jasper — ridiculously good.

Maisie and Toby are examples of dog resilience, the ability under the right conditions to bounce back from sometimes questionable or horrific circumstances and become "good dogs."

They are a lesson for us. We, too, can be resilient, able to "bounce back" from difficult situations. We have grit. Like dogs, it takes some work.

Here are six ways you can help foster resilience in your dog, though these can also help anyone bounce back from difficulty. These are lessons I've learned from watching our dogs, and ones I've adapted from a groundbreaking paper by Margaret Haglund and Nicole Cooper, "Six Keys to Resilience for PTSD and Everyday Stress."

1. *Active coping:* In the case of our dogs, we knew they were stressed. Beyond just being guardians, we had to make efforts and take time to help them destress. For humans, active coping means having a conscious way to deal with everyday and acute stress.
2. *Physical exercise:* This is important for both dogs and humans. Hiking, walking, and play improves mood

and health. With a stressed dog, the more exercise the better.

3. *A positive attitude:* "Optimism is moral courage," wrote Ernest Shackleton. For our dogs, positive reinforcement, with minimal if any punishment, is vital to let them know they are in a loving environment. Punishing can cause fear; for a stressed dog, it probably brings back bad memories.

4. *Social support:* Individuals who have lots of social support, who have a sense of belonging, tend to be more resilient. Same for stressed dogs. Toby and Maisie let us know when they need alone time. The rest of the time, most of their existence, they want to be with us. Plus, the more dogs can socialize, the calmer they are around people. A golden rule for a new dog or one with a possibly sketchy history is to not leave them alone for more than a few hours at a time. Be cautious about crates. For some dogs, a crate can be a trigger.

5. *Patience:* I can't say this enough: It takes time for a dog to go from scared and stressed to happy. Stuff will happen, you'll get frustrated. Be patient. Be kind and loving. Dogs evolved (and we evolved) to be together. Sometimes it just takes time.

6. *Help from experts:* Remember, you don't have to do everything yourself. There are amazing dog trainers and individuals who specialize in dog behavior (I don't mean dog psychics). Reach out, stay informed, read, learn as much as you can. My own opinion is to avoid trainers who use punishment as a tool.

Maisie and Toby Versus the Coyotes

"Hey," I yelled, with both my arms up. "Get outta here!"

I was shouting at two coyotes who were trailing us on our morning walk. They were about fifty feet behind us. Toby and Maisie were straining at their leashes and barking like mad. Toby wanted to be let loose. Coyotes are his natural enemy. Ten thousand years of evolution protecting sheep has hardwired that instinct.

Maisie, on the other hand, while brave, is not the smartest when it comes to coyote encounters. She was the reason they were following us. Small dogs often fall prey to coyotes.

She put up a good show. I did get the feeling that while Toby wanted to go for them, Maisie, while growling and barking up a storm, was sending me the psychic message: *Hold me back!*

It was September, when coyotes are active, and it was early in the morning, when the wild world is up and about.

New Mexico has a split personality when it comes to coyotes. On the one hand, there are the ranchers and hunters who think of them as pests and predators. There used to be coyote killing contests every year until the voice of the urban and suburban populations weighed in and the contests were made illegal on state-owned lands.

In the community we live in, coyotes are tolerated, even celebrated. There are road signs with the message: "Thank you for watching out for our coyotes." There are community presentations on not using poison for mice because coyotes eat mice, and the poison goes up the food chain, sometimes killing the coyotes.

I'm with the tolerating crowd. One of my favorite times on the fire department was when, at night, we turned on our sirens to go to a call and were answered by the howls of coyotes all around us.

Yet on that morning, as those two coyotes tracked us, I felt a bit nervous.

The thing about coyotes is that they seem so relaxed. Their gait is easy, their demeanor calm. In the act of pursuing, it is as if they're saying, we do this every day. Mice, rabbits, pack rats, cats, little dogs. It's all the same to us. In Northern California a while ago, an individual was attacked by a mountain lion. Although he ultimately fought it off, he couldn't help but notice how calm the lion was — *I'm the predator, you're the prey. This is something I do daily. It's the circle of life, buddy.*

As they got closer, I picked up a few rocks. I have lousy aim, exacerbated by the fact that I was trying to hold back two deranged dogs. I did finally throw one rock and missed, but I spooked the coyotes, and they headed up an arroyo.

As you can imagine, the dogs, the leashes, and I were all tangled up. In trying to spin around and untangle us, I let go of Maisie's leash.

Whoops.

Sensing freedom, in not her brightest move, she sprinted away, trailing her leash, barking madly, up the arroyo in pursuit of the two coyotes.

"Shit!" I yelled.

I had only one recourse: *Release the kraken!* Imagining myself as Liam Neeson (as Zeus) in *Clash of the Titans*, I let Toby go.

He galloped up the arroyo with me stumbling and running after him.

I could hear Maisie's bark, but Toby was silent. I imagined him determinedly focused on catching a coyote. I cut around a cactus and scrambled up the slope. After a minute or so, I couldn't hear Maisie. I called her name: nothing.

I worried that her leash would get caught on a tree or rocks and she'd be a sitting duck for the coyotes.

Finally, out of breath, hands on my knees, I tried to figure out what to do next. My only option was to continue up the arroyo and hope that Maisie had stayed in the drainage.

I headed up. I yelled her name.

A moment later she came bursting around a tree and came right to me, jumping up. If she could've talked, I'm sure she would've told me how brave she was to chase the coyotes away from her human.

What about Toby? I was confident that one or two coyotes would run from him, but if he encountered a pack, it could be trouble. I yelled his name, but he had taken off into miles of piñon and juniper forest. He could be anywhere and not hear me.

When Toby didn't show up, I decided to go back to the road, take Maisie home, and then go on the hunt for him.

As we made our way down the arroyo, my phone rang. It was our neighbor, who lived about a half mile from us. She said Toby had just trotted through their yard and was headed back toward the road. I thanked her profusely and headed toward their house.

Within a few minutes, Toby popped out of the brush and trotted over to Maisie and me on the road. He was out of breath, but his demeanor said, *Mischief sorted!*

We walked back to our house, both dogs acting triumphant. At home, Maisie jumped up on Laurie and wagged her tail. I'm sure she was trying to convey the whole story of the hundred coyotes she had single-handedly defeated that day. The stuff of legends. (Like me, an exaggerator.) Toby, more blasé, just jumped up on the couch. It was a normal day for his kin.

Afterward, my views on coyotes didn't change much, despite encountering a pair who stalked us. How would I feel if a coyote had grabbed Maisie? I'd like to believe I'd be shocked, terrified, and sad, but I wouldn't buy a gun. The truth is I want to see coyotes on our walks. I was awestruck when a mountain lion banged into our kitchen door (see page 164). I didn't love it, but I was awestruck, even as she stared into my soul. I want to witness the flyover of sandhill cranes heading north from the Bosque del Apache wildlife refuge. I want to live in a world where we accommodate and celebrate the wild, even when it's inconvenient. In my view, a few national parks doesn't cut it. Even if I never visit certain places, I want to know that wilderness is there.

I fear mine is a minority opinion. I know many ranchers and farmers want to reduce predation from predators, which impacts their livelihood. And I know pets and humans need to be protected, as much as possible, from the extremely rare attacks by predators, be they grizzlies, mountain lions, wolves, or coyotes.

I don't agree with the vociferous group that wishes we could rid our continent of predators entirely, or of any animals they deem as "pests," using traps, poison, shooting contests. As a teenager, I was driving to visit a friend in February on a rural road, and from my car I witnessed five or so individuals, adults and teenagers, on snowmobiles chasing a terrorized fox through deep snow. Some people see animals as "things" that are worth nothing except to be hunted and killed.

All that said, our coyote encounter reinforced my commitment to take simple precautions on our walks. We don't walk in the evening or early morning, when coyotes are most active. Most importantly, I am "situationally aware," focused on the walk, not on my phone or listening to podcasts or other distractions. This is how we need to be in areas where humans and dogs live close to wilderness (or I suppose on busy streets). I look around and pay attention to the dogs. When they stop and their ears perk up, I look and listen. Toby, because he was bred to protect sheep from coyotes and wolves, is our bellwether. He is constantly on the lookout for coyotes. He howls when he hears them, lunges when he sees them. He is the perfect dog to walk with on our wild road.

Bravery

The rest of that week I couldn't help thinking about bravery and dogs. Except for our two German shepherds bolting back into the house at the sight of a bear, all our dogs, and maybe yours, too, have this quality of being brave. They exhibit the willingness to risk being hurt, or even killed, to protect us. Even Maisie, who should know better, wanted to go after those coyotes rather than sprint back to the house.

Part of this no doubt evolved from the "protect the pack at all costs" mentally of ancient wolves, thus giving individual wolves and the pack the best shot at passing on genes. Once humans and dogs became "partners," no doubt the other part is human selection and training dogs to be protective. Yet does any of that take away from the individual dog's choice in the moment to go after a pair of coyotes or stare down strangers who appear at the doorstep?

We don't know what is going on in the minds of dogs. Are they actually fearless, or are they afraid yet still willing to take the risk, to act — to bolt up an arroyo when they know they're outnumbered?

Think of us. After all, we evolved in much the same way, in small hunter-gatherer groups, where being in and protecting the tribe was paramount for passing on our genes.

For us, because we can reflect on it and hear stories of

others doing brave things, we know that being brave isn't about being fearless. Rather, it is acting, doing the right thing, even when we're terrified. Could it be the same with our dogs? That in those moments, even though they are acting bravely, they are also scared? I think so. Fear and bravery go hand in hand. We can't experience bravery without fear.

I gather from this a couple of lessons. First, we are both, human and dog, inherently brave. Dogs react to anything perceived as dangerous, be it a tree blowing in the wind or a blind date coming to our apartment. (Rule: If your dog doesn't like your date, immediately dump them.)

For us it is much more complicated. Most of the time, we rarely find ourselves in life-or-death situations.

Yet bravery is required. It might not be the "defending the family" kind of bravery, but it takes bravery — to act even when we're scared — to get on in life. For example, choosing to do hard things rather than taking the easy path. It takes bravery to ask someone out, to say "I love you" more often, to admit we're wrong, to apologize. It takes bravery to deal with the inevitables: trauma, sickness, and death. To go our own way, speak our truth, and so on. To thrive requires courage.

And courage is our birthright. We wouldn't be here if generations of our ancestors weren't incredibly brave. That courage is in us, too; we just sometimes must call it forth and practice it. Sometimes we need to ask, when we come up to something scary or difficult, "What is the bravest thing I can do?" Then take the tremulous steps forward, despite anxiety or fear. That's being brave.

Our dogs remind us of this. Watch how their ears go up when they sense danger. Watch how alert they become. Watch how they are instantly willing to challenge anything that might be a threat: to step in front of us to save our lives. Our challenges and threats might be a world different, but we have the same courage within.

Part 6

Final Lessons

We will always be one animal wondering about the emotional experience of another animal.

— Laurel Braitman

Bonnie (my dad's dog), Shawnee, Rikka, Max, Alyosha, Riva, Nugie, Zuni, Sombra, Oso, Mowgli, Jamaica, Nellie, Tank, Maisie, and Toby...and of course, Tallulah and now Letty.

Over sixty years, those were (and are) the dogs of our lives. We've loved them and they have been the teachers of important lessons.

They have been the best kind of teachers. They teach by just being themselves — dogs. No artifice, no theories; they pass on wisdom just by being.

In the summer of 2022, my daughter Brynne adopted another dog, a rescue Cavalier King Charles spaniel named Letty. She was less than two years old (we think) when adopted, and Letty hit the ground ready to teach. Brynne sent a video a month or so after Letty arrived. She was playing with Brynne's eighteen-month-old son, Dash. Letty assumes the play position, and Dash squeals in delight. Letty runs a circle around him and repeats. Dash chases, wobbling as he runs, and Letty stays just out of reach. First life lesson: how to play. Dash will grow up bonded to Letty. Letty will be by his side as he explores, comes home from school, and (hopefully) goes on magical walks in the woods by their house.

For all the teaching dogs do, the last part of this book is about what we owe them. Dogs have moral standing. Dogs are not just "pets" but are and can be a vital part of our lives and our learning about life. The simple act of walking with a dog can teach us about our connection to the wild and natural world. And as we cross the "very narrow bridge," a dog can offer us companionship, making sure we are not alone in our great, wonderful, tragic, and astonishing journey.

Fourteen thousand years ago, in Germany, an adult couple was buried with two dogs. The woman's hand was found resting on the head of one of the dogs. The author of the research paper noted, "There must be a story there."

For me the story is this: Since before there were cities and agriculture, dogs and humans have been together, bonded. We have evolved to care for each other. At night, when Toby jumps up on the couch and settles in next to me, and I put my hand on his head, I think about that ancient woman and her dog: We are the same. We loved a dog.

The Trial of the Pig

In fifteenth-century France, in the village of Falaise, a mother pig (a sow) and her five piglets were put on trial for killing a five-year-old boy.

A lot to unpack.

First, for context, if that happened today, the pig would've been euthanized — our more polite word for killing — without much ado. Mostly likely, we'd give two typical justifications for killing the pig: first, revenge, to assuage the anger and sorrow of the parents (although no act by people or gods can assuage the death of a child); and second, to prevent the "child-killer" sow from killing again. We often assume that once an animal kills a human, they will likely do it again. Once a tiger, wolf, alligator, bear, or mountain lion tastes human flesh, we believe they will become human predators, "man-eaters." But of course, we also have the justification of the Old Testament (whether you are religious or not). It has hung in the air since before Christ and in every age since, a warning about any violent act — whether human- or animal-caused: "Who so sheddeth man's blood, by man shall his blood be shed."

According to records, the trial was a solemn affair. There was a prosecutor, a defense attorney for the pig, a judge, and eyewitnesses. As was custom, the pig was held in a cage, like a human prisoner, in the courtroom. If the sow had squealed or grunted during the proceedings, she might have found herself in contempt for disrupting the proceedings.

Because the pig was a domestic animal, the trial was secular. During this era, issues with wild animals, including moles, rats, and insects that destroyed crops, were handled by ecclesiastical courts. Those animals were tried and often punished by banishment or by being cursed. I have no idea how you banish moles.

In essence, medieval courts assigned moral reasoning to animals and even to insects.

In this sow's case, she was found guilty because, according to the court, she made the choice to attack the child. She had the intent to attack, and she chose to do it. The piglets, on the other hand, even though they were "blood spattered," did not have the ability to form intent and were thus found innocent.

The sow was tortured and executed. The piglets presumably were sent back to the owner, who suffered no consequences other than the loss of his pig.

Although pigs were commonly found guilty of crimes — they were basically free-ranging in medieval villages — donkeys, the occasional chicken (one chicken was tried for laying a "cursed egg"), cows, and of course dogs also found themselves tangled up in the legal system of the time. The trial outcomes for attacking or killing a human or another valuable animal most often resulted in torture and death.

If this seems mind-boggling, I'm right there with you.

Scholars tend to focus on a couple of reasons for animal trials. One, all life belonged to a Divine Order. During sixth grade in Catholic school, I was taught that order:

God — pope — divinely "appointed" kings — commoners (my Irish family) — animals — plants. Any disruption of that order was serious and must be dealt with — a pig killing a human was unacceptable, and the pig had to be tried and punished.

Other modern scholars seem to just throw their hands up. The fifteenth century was a primitive and superstitious time.

Different times and different cultures "hold" animals in their lives and imaginations in ways that may seem bizarre to us, yet there are interesting ideas to explore.

In light of the sow's trial, the question I'd like to consider is: What is the correct moral standing for animals? If animals are morally responsible for their actions, then the medieval animal trials might make some kind of weird sense. On the other hand, to what extent are we morally responsible for how we treat animals? Throughout history, how people have answered these questions has depended a lot on when and where they have lived.

In the United States today, 99 percent of the animals we consume for food are raised on factory farms. We slaughter approximately 10 billion animals a year. Nor do we have a lot of close contact with those animals. On factory farms, animals have numbers, not names.

In medieval times, European villagers lived closely with their animals, be they animals to be slaughtered for meat or chickens and cows that provided eggs and milk. Free-roaming cats kept vermin at bay, and village dogs ate scraps and were burglar alarm systems.

While today we only tend to cuddle with our dogs on cold winter nights, William Manchester, in his book *A World*

Lit Only by Fire, wrote that medieval families and their dogs, pigs, cats, and chickens all occasionally slept together in a communal heap in a small and barely heated hut.

Each day was spent with animals. Medieval villagers knew all their animals — they lived with them, fed them, guarded them, and watched or helped as mothers delivered calves, piglets, puppies, kittens, eggs. They cleaned up after their animals and butchered them when the time was right.

To the medieval farmer's discerning eye, all living creatures shared birth, life, and death. And birth and death looked the same whether dog, cow, or human. If that was true, why not believe that the mental processes, how beings made choices, were also similar?

Based on their observations, it made perfect sense to assume that pigs, dogs, and other animals made and acted on moral choices. This was no doubt unabashed anthropomorphizing, but why wouldn't they? There was no psychology professor telling them not to. Using the tools of intimate observation and intuition, they saw animals making choices every day, and thus, like humans, those animals had to live by the consequences of those decisions. A pig who chose to kill a human should be brought to trial, as a human would be, so that all could see how the pig's choice brought her to grief. A lesson for everyone, pig and human.

Of course, then the Enlightenment happened. The scientific revolution exalted rationality, and animal trials came to be seen as, what is the word I want to use?

Nonsensical.

Today, to our twenty-first-century selves, with all our science and technology, these trials seem foolish, backward, ignorant. The science historian Thomas Goldstein scolds us for that presumption. He writes, "It is a mark of modern ignorance to think that we have become smarter.... Who is to say that the task of tackling a problem without the benefit of a well-developed body of methods and information may not have required far greater intellectual vigor and originality...? Prehistoric, early historic, as well as medieval science have faced such a task."

Medieval Europeans came to conclusions about the moral reasoning of animals that fit their experience. Enlightenment scientists like Ivan Pavlov came to different conclusions. In part because of his classical conditioning experiments with dogs (which, shockingly, he also conducted with orphaned children), dogs were reimagined, in our collective consciousness, as stimulus-response machines. Rather than choice-making beings, animals were "black boxes" where inputs (like the ringing of a bell) caused a predictable output: salivation.

In my opinion, neither medieval nor Enlightenment views are accurate, yet both hold kernels of truth. As a dog curls up on our lap, or excitedly runs up and down the hallway in anticipation of a run, we know, *we know*, that the dog understands and can make choices and possesses their own sense of right and wrong.

Recent scientific research supports this conclusion. Dogs are constantly making choices, though we often can only surmise the reasons. Why did Toby drive those coyotes away from Maisie and me? I can speculate about why (and one reason might be evolved, hardwired instinct, a stimulus response), but ultimately I can't prove what's correct. Another example is when Toby goes from sound asleep to roaring out the dog door, then comes in and jumps back on the couch: I have no idea why he does that.

On the other hand, the medieval idea that dogs possess the same moral reasoning as humans is a stretch. If dogs had their own courts, they could put themselves on trial for any dog crimes, but we can't hold dogs to human moral standards and charge them with human crimes. Nor can dogs punish us for what they might consider our crimes against dogdom — if they did, we'd get five to ten for every leash, fence, and crate.

Here is where I land. Whatever dogs know, whatever ethical concepts they possess, they are aware, emotional beings. For that reason alone, they possess, as Yale philosophy professor Shelly Kagan describes it, "moral standing."

Philosopher Mary Anne Warren provided this definition: "To have moral status is to be morally considerable, or to have moral standing....If an entity has moral status, then we may not treat it in just any way we please."

We cannot treat dogs, or any sentient being, in just any way we please.

A lot to unpack. We live in a paradoxical world. The issue is not just about our dog, but the entire species. On the one hand, I treasure my time with Maisie and Toby, I love them. Laurie and I think about their needs and spoil them. I think most dog guardians feel and act the same way.

On the other hand, thousands of dogs are used for medical experiments every year, and they are not treated in a way that is "morally considerable." Over the last century, researchers have conducted numerous "inhumane" experiments, ones that cause pain and suffering (like Martin Seligman's "learned helplessness" experiments), in order to confirm what medieval peoples already knew: Dogs feel pain and suffer. Further, we would be horrified if "our dog" was ever subjected to the abusive protocols that thousands of beagles used in research are put through every year.

Abandoned dogs are another moral problem. In 2020, over 6.5 million pets were turned over to shelters, although this is down from 1973, when 20 million pets were given away. Of those 6.5 million abandoned pets in 2020, only about half were adopted, and only 28 percent of dogs. Over 650,000 dogs are euthanized annually.

It's important to remember that shelters are not a dog problem, they're a human problem. As the dog cognition scientist Alexandra Horowitz wrote, "A shelter doesn't shelter dogs, it shelters irresponsible people."

I ask myself, often late at night, how does this paradox exist? We live in a world that idolizes dogs (I obviously do), *and* we destroy and discard them at will. We give "moral consideration" to that singular dog staring back at us in a shelter, the one we adopt, but we often treat other beings as if they have no moral standing at all.

This is as cruel and irrational as putting a pig on trial.

I have reached an uncomfortable place for a Minnesotan. I don't like telling others what to do. I am not some flaming sword of judgment. Yet this paradox is the elephant in the room, seen but undiscussable.

Here are the actions and standards I try to hold myself to:

1. Our pets have moral standing, so we can't treat them like "property."
2. Dogs (and all pets) are a lifetime commitment.
3. If possible, try to adopt dogs from a shelter.
4. Newly adopted rescue animals require patience. It takes time for a terrified animal to adjust to new humans.
5. Volunteering at a shelter is one way to live with higher purpose. Shelters always need the help, and the reward is priceless: grateful dogs (and cats, rabbits, parrots, and any other animal).

Dogs of Ukraine

How we have intellectually held animals over the last five hundred years has evolved from putting animals on trial to seeing them as simply "stimulus-response" vehicles to now a reframing of our relationships with all living things as we look around and daily discover sentience.

I began this book describing how, when I was young, it was common in rural Minnesota for individuals to throw unwanted puppies into the river. I believe — because I want to believe and we are seeing evidence — that there's been a shift in our collective conscience since then. More importantly, we are moving toward accepting how vital dogs are to our lives.

As one vivid example, consider the dogs of Ukraine.

This story isn't just about dogs, however. It's about the choices we make during the most terrible crises we may ever face: war, natural disaster, or any deadly threat that forces us to flee, taking only what we can carry.

For historical context:

In 1939, just before Germany invaded Poland, fear of war broke out across Europe. The horrors of the Great War were still vivid and fresh. In England, the National Air Raid Precautions Animals Committee (NARPAC) circulated a pamphlet with advice for animal owners. It read, "If at all possible, send or take your household animals into the country in advance of an emergency....If you cannot place them in the care of neighbors, it really is kindest to have them destroyed."

In the following week, almost 750,000 pets were, in their words, "culled" or abandoned at shelters.

The prewar mantra: "Evacuate the children, put up the blackout curtains, kill the cat."

Fast-forward to Ukraine. Between February and April 2022 — only seventy-seven years after the end of World War II, a single lifetime — Russia invaded the country (and the war remains ongoing as I write). One of the untold stories is how the initial invasion affected the lives of pet guardians and their animals. Ukraine is a pet-loving country: Before the war, it was home to 750,000 dogs and 5.5 million cats.

Then, on February 24, 2022, the invasion began with Russian rockets raining down on Ukrainian cities — cities just like ours. On that horrific day, families had to make the choice: Do we stay or run for our lives? If we flee, what do we take?

If we have never been in a similar situation, it can be hard to put ourselves in someone else's shoes. A people being invaded faces the loss of everything — their homes and livelihoods, their nation, their plans and hopes. As James Baldwin wrote, "The breakup of the world as one has always known it, the loss of all that gave one an identity, the end of safety." People panic, and fearing for their lives, make choices they might not make in any other circumstance. We must remember to suspend judgment. In England before war broke out, people anticipated bombings and food shortages; they knew scores of domestic pets would be abandoned. Some saw killing pets as both a mercy and necessary for personal survival.

Ukraine is also a modern country filled with people who love their pets, walk their dogs, and treat them as family. In the early days of the war, as broadcasts showed vivid images of millions of people, now labeled refugees, leaving their country, I was struck by the number of individuals carrying their pets: dogs, cats, and even a few canaries. I watched a video of a family walking along a road with thousands of other war refugees. Able to bring only what they could carry, the father had hoisted a young husky puppy on his shoulders. I dreamed of being that family. What if that was me carrying Maisie, holding Toby on a leash, as we left everything we knew and shuffled toward the unknown with only ourselves, a few necessities, and our pets?

In a research paper on the Ukrainian evacuations, scholars looked at 115 pet-owning families from Kyiv. Most evacuated. About 40 percent stayed behind, and one of the reasons given was the need to take care of their pets. These are the people photographed in front of bombed and burned-out buildings, staring in shock and holding a dog on a leash.

The study noted that only seven families left their pets as they evacuated. A few told researchers they had been out of the country when the attack happened; others had to be urgently evacuated in the face of an imminent attack by Russian troops, especially in Bucha, a suburb of Kyiv. One of the factors that facilitated people choosing to leave Ukraine with their pets was that Ukrainian authorities were allowing pets on trains and buses, and surrounding countries like Poland were allowing animals in, no questions asked. The researchers found that families who evacuated with their pets showed an increase in well-being compared to those without pets.

As I did, I think we all wonder what we'd do if we faced a similar crisis. How would we deal with the dilemma of taking or leaving our dogs? In truth, we can't know until the moment comes. Circumstances can make our choice for us. But it's a healthy exercise to put yourself in that moment and consider.

You never know when a life-threatening crisis might arise. In New Mexico, we live in "fire country," where wildfires in the spring and summer are increasingly common. Actually, because of climate change and the Southwest's mega-drought, wildfires are getting closer to a year-round thing. In the mountains, firefighters now tramp through snow to get to fires. Our house is surrounded by extremely dry and thus explosive piñon and juniper. We are vulnerable to losing our house and having to evacuate quickly if we see smoke billowing from any direction. Thus, we have a "go list." It's posted on our hallway wall. It's a short list of the things we need and can quickly throw in our cars and get out.

It reads: *Dogs first.*

Everything else can be replaced, but our living, breathing, sentient nonhuman partners cannot. *We love them.* As I watched the unfolding tragedy in Ukraine and the courage and care the Ukrainians have for their pets, I knew they were me, and I them, and we'd make the same obvious, unarguable choice.

Walking in the Universe

People say that walking on water is a miracle,
but to me, walking peacefully on the Earth is the real miracle.
The Earth is a miracle. Each step is a miracle.

— THICH NHAT HANH

This book is about the lessons that dogs teach us. And I have found that walking peacefully on the earth with dogs is, and I don't use this word lightly, a profound experience...if we pay attention.

It's a seemingly mundane everyday experience, walking the dogs, often along the same roads, streets, or trails. Joseph Campbell, the mythologist, wrote about finding our bliss. Now, mine is daily rediscovered in walking with Toby and Maisie.

I want to explain the sacredness of the walk.

That starts with redefining *sacred*. I want to borrow it from theological connotations and use it in the larger context of *connectedness*. We — all beings on earth — are connected. This is the most sacred understanding.

We can consider it from an evolutionary point of view. There is a common tree of life that we all belong to — bacteria to human. We share DNA up and down the tree. Four simple substances make up the DNA of all living things, adenine, thymine, guanine, and cytosine.

Or we can consider it from an Indigenous point of view. From a First People's perspective, according to one encapsulation, "Everyone and everything has a purpose, is worthy of respect and caring, and has a place in the grand scheme of life." Evolution and Indigenous beliefs are not in conflict. Rather, they are so complementary it gives me goose bumps.

So, how does a walk with dogs rise to the sacred?

Let's start with a perspective shift.

It involves taking a walk at night, away from city lights.

Our lovely daylight blue and cloudy skies mask a reality. The reality, which is clearly on display at night, is the vastness and unknowability of the universe. It isn't the billions of stars in our galaxy that I see, or the seemingly infinite number of stars in the universe. Rather, the darkness between it all, that immeasurable space, draws my attention. Dark. Cold. Empty. (I know, it's not truly "empty," there's dark matter and dark energy, and maybe more.)

Then I see pictures taken from the moon of our little blue-green-brown planet, enveloped in an atmosphere, and I am full of wonder. It is extraordinary. That we exist here is the definition of miraculous. That should be the benchmark for miraculous. The word *miraculous* should not be used to describe anything else.

I realize that Maisie, Toby, and I are not just walking down the same road every day. We are walking on a planet, a planet teeming with ancient life — all evolved from the same single-cell creatures four billion years ago — in a distant arm of the Milky Way in a universe that seems beyond our comprehension.

With that perspective, we start our daily ritual: under the sky, the moon, the stars, and the universe.

I can only assume from our dogs' behavior that going out the door for that walk is the singular event of their day. As I open the door and they strain on their leashes (and I am sorry they're on leashes!), I wonder, what is it they want to learn?

Before we've even left our driveway, they are excitedly smelling the stack of cuttings that Laurie places in our mulch pile. Then they pull me down the driveway, impatient to dive into the dozens of scents wafting along our road. Dozens? Hundreds. The scents left by other dogs, coyote markings. The blue grama grasses along the road must be explored. A beetle scuttles close to Maisie's paws. I point out a stick bug and a praying mantis. The mantis rotates her head as she watches us walk by. (Some summers, I've done a daily beetle count; long story.) Crows call out our approach. Toby stops and looks up. Piñon jays scatter from their roosts in the trees, jabbering at us in annoyance. In the morning, birds perch at the top of the junipers, and ponderosas soak in the heat of the rising sun. A pair of mourning doves flits by. We might see rattlesnakes, cottontails, mule and white-tailed deer, multitudes of wildflowers and grasses. Across a fence, longhorn cattle lift their heads and watch us pass.

This is the high desert! Life is everywhere and we are connected to it. In the web of life, everything has a purpose and is part of the ecology of the planet.

Our dogs help me *see* all this. It starts with their curiosity, their need to inspect every little thing on a walk and then do it again the next day.

Walking with a three-year-old human child is the same. They are intensely curious. My granddaughter Fiona, at three, once followed a singular beetle in our yard, and I hope her curiosity will drive her to want to know more about beetles. The species is nearly 300 million years old. Every fourth species on earth is a beetle. They are the world's decomposers. Every being has a purpose.

Follow a dog or a child, explore a little, ask one question, which leads to another, and then a whole new world appears before you. Children and dogs.

On a walk, the most important thing to do is be curious. We walk for all sorts of reasons. We decompress. We count steps. We listen to music. We make lists. If we are not alone, we talk.

Yet if we follow our dog's nose, if we spend a bit of time wondering about where that plant, that flower, that mysterious jackrabbit — their head and ears peeking out from a bush — came from, and we do it repeatedly, the biosphere emerges before us as astonishing and interconnected.

We walk in a sacred space. Life connected, life dependent. Nothing stands, walks, runs, creeps, swims, slithers, sends out shoots or roots independently. Every living creature has a past, a history that takes it back to those single-cell ancestors four billion years ago.

It is the great Oneness.

A note: This is more difficult in cities. That's a problem. Although it is hard to apply the word *downtown* to Santa

Fe, on one street near town, there is a hollyhock, one of the biggest and healthiest I've seen here, that grows out of a crack in the sidewalk.

Life is everywhere. We need only to be curious and look.

Of course, our dogs don't give a whit about the biosphere or connectedness. They live in it, they exist because of it, and they are forever curious about it, but abstract thought is not their strong suit.

It is up to us. A dog can point us to a living thing, they can root around a prairie sunflower (while we hurriedly look up its genus on our iPhone). It is up to us to make the connections and teach others, to, in the poet Mary Oliver's words, "pay attention, be amazed, tell about it."

And so we walk, and I learn. Our road follows the contours of hills and a wide arroyo carved by a millennia of flash floods. Down in the arroyo, the wind dies down, the temperature is cooler. There is shade in the summer. Maisie pulls me from shady patch to shady patch; Toby, head down, smelling his way, follows behind.

Cars drive by, they bark. People and dogs walk by, they tug at their leashes and bark. Then we are again alone.

We climb up the final hill to our house. They both bark at our neighbor's dog, another daily ritual. Then we are home.

It seems a bit comedic to make claims about the universe from a simple walk with dogs around a one-mile looping road in Santa Fe, New Mexico. Yet we have big skies and the horizons are hundreds of miles away. This land has been tramped on by humans for almost twenty thousand years. It's conducive to wonder. All the principles of biology, of chemistry and physics, are on display along our little communal road. A walk there is rarely boring. I hope it is the same for you on your road.

Be curious. Pay attention. Be amazed.

When There Is Nothing to Do, It's Okay to Do Nothing

THE WORLD IS A VERY NARROW BRIDGE

Last chapter. Before I sat down to write this, I took Toby to one of the big dog parks in Santa Fe. Maisie is a bit too small to go; the park is huge and there are big dogs. Maisie is understandably nervous around strange big dogs.

I took off Toby's leash (off-leash!), and we wandered. During the entire walk, he mostly stuck right by my side or just behind me on the narrower trails. I'm still at the point where — with Toby's history — it squeezes my heart a bit to have him stick so close to me.

I'm fairly certain he was trying to send me the psychic message: *Don't screw up the last chapter!* I talk to him about the book a lot, so he's up to speed on how important a last chapter can be.

No pressure.

This last chapter is about a song.

It's an Israeli pop song. The lyrics date back to the eighteenth century and Rabbi Nachman of Breslov. The full lyric is "The whole entire world is a very narrow bridge, and the main thing is to have no fear at all." It was made into a song and broadcast over Israeli radio during the Yom Kippur War in 1973.

To it, I add, "Cross it with a dog."

Let me explain.

The whole entire world is a very narrow bridge.

It is narrow, old, and rickety. In the middle, it sags. In a big wind it shakes so bad it could toss you off into the chasm below. You cannot see the other side of the bridge. It is hidden in the mist.

But, and this is important, the view of the chasm is beautiful. It is not to be missed; it will feed your soul.

There is no way to cross the chasm except this thousands-of-years-old bridge. We — you and I — have no choice but to cross it. That is why we are *here*.

And let's be clear. We get only one attempt, that's the rub, that's what no one tells you when you are young.

One crossing, one life.

Of course, billions of humans have crossed it before us, yet that is cold comfort for our crossing.

Our crossing is the most intimate of strivings.

As it sways in the breeze and a first step is taken, it buckles. You freeze. You want to lay down, hold on, and not move.

Yet a voice from inside whispers, we are not built to freeze. We are built to cross the bridge. It's in our DNA, it's in every fiber of every story told, of every experience shared: We are to cross the bridge.

The obstacle is fear.

The main thing is to have no fear at all.

My friends, we will all cross the bridge. The choice is, do we cross it terrified of every step, anxious about every choice? Are we full of recriminations about past steps? Do we come up with hundreds of reasons not to take the next step? Or can we summon the courage to move, stride, dance, and help others as they cross — and enjoy the view?

Every day we have the choice. Day by day. Step by step.

Cross it with a dog.

Today, walking with Toby by my side, I had this ineffable sense of lightness, of companionship. Even though it was early, and there were few others in the park, I felt I wasn't alone.

When I was young and bold, I thought that being alone, in the woods, in the streets, in my first apartment, was a sure sign of becoming an adult: understanding what life was about — in other words, how to cross that bridge.

In my young brain it went without saying: We cross it alone! I was, as is typical of a twenty-something contemplating big thoughts in America, wrong.

We are built to cross the bridge, and we evolved not to be alone while we cross it.

Toby walked by my side, smelling what there was to smell and regularly looking up at me. Toby's glance crossed the chasm of different species: We are together, we are meant to walk this earth, this bridge, at this time, together.

Evolution is what brought us to this point.

What a gift!

We should remember that evolution is the Uncle Scrooge of gift-giving. As the writer Annie Dillard wrote in *Pilgrim at Tinker Creek*, "Evolution loves death more than it loves you or me.... The universe that suckled us is a monster that does not care if we live or die — does not care if itself grinds to a halt. It is fixed and blind, a robot programmed to kill. We are free and seeing, we can only try to outwit it at every turn to save our skins."

We have, by twists of fate, by maybe a generous hominid and an inquisitive wolf, been given this evolutionary gift of companionship to help us outwit the evolutionary monster.

What does it mean to have a dog with us on our journey? It is to know that if you are kind, and giving, you get back enthusiastic love. You get the love of a dog (or dogs) who greet you daily at the door, who are so happy to see you. You get the devotion of an animal that will give their life for their human companion.

No matter how tough your day was, how beaten down you might feel, they are there for one thing: to be with you.

Living in an amoral universe, let's celebrate this gift of companionship.

Of course, we also need humans! As *Homo sapiens*, we crave companionship and love. It's not either/or, it's both/and. I dive into the world of family and friends. I am nurtured by them. When I close my eyes, I see a line of people holding hands crossing the bridge. There is a Yiddish saying, "Life is with people." And so it is. I also see, weaving in and out of that line of people, dogs, our partners for thousands of years.

On our walk, Toby was nonchalant about all this. I could see it in his relaxed gait. He's not one to worry about existential ideas, be they in a song or his guardian's angst. And, most notably, when we arrived home, he was immediately up on the couch, paws over the edge, asleep and snoring.

(When there is nothing to do, it's okay to do nothing.)

I knew that as he slept, and Laurie and Sully and I talked in the kitchen, he could hear us. The sound of his family. We talked about changing his food. Sully implored me to look at how cute he was, and how Maisie, our little one, was cuddled up next to him — all we could see was her head peering at us over the couch.

And Toby dreamed: We are crossing the narrow bridge. On a leash he leads me. I am ten and I am seventy. I reach my hand out to touch his head.

"Good dog, Toby, good boy."

"Retriever" by Barbara Crooker

If "Heaven is a lovely lake of beer" as St. Bridget wrote,
then dog heaven must be this tub of kibble, where you can push
your muzzle all day long without getting bloat or bellyache,
Where every toilet seat is raised, at the right level
for slurping and fire hydrant and saplings tell you, "Here.
Relieve yourself on us." And the sun and moon
fall at your feet, celestial frisbees flinging themselves
in shining arcs for your soft mouth to retrieve. Rumi says,
"Personality is a small dog trying to get the soul to play,"
but you are a big dog, with an even larger heart, and you
have redeemed our better selves. Forgive us for the times
we walked away, wanted to do taxes or wash dishes
instead of playing fetch or tugger. In the green field
of heaven, there are no collars, no leashes, no delivery trucks
with bad brakes, and all the dogs run free. Barking is allowed,
and every pocket holds a treat. Sit. Stay. Good dog.

ACKNOWLEDGMENTS

I grew up believing that to be a writer meant hours of slaving over a typewriter by yourself in a badly lit room. Coffee and cigarettes your only companions. Humans banished! Nothing could be further from the truth. Writing a book is a collaborative act (and I have never smoked!). Writers, at least this one, need help, they need readers, individuals with honest critiques, and family members who are patient and forgiving when asked for the nth time to reread the same paragraph.

I have had amazing readers: Terrie Pitts in Nova Scotia, Tracy Burke in Denver, Linda Pedelty and Sandra Jaramillo in Santa Fe.

My partner Laurie, our daughters Brynne and Sully, have lent emotional support and that familial critique about my use of *lay* or *lie*. Hurtful, but useful. And of course, our dogs, all of them, alive or passed, have given me a gift that is immeasurable.

About the artwork in the book. The drawings are from my great friend and fire department mentor, the astonishing Southwest artist Dan Bodelson. His remarkable work can be seen at DanBodelson.com.

Lastly, the professionals at New World Library. Jason Gardner, my editor and guide, and Jeff Campbell, an amazing and generous copyeditor. Thank you, thank you!

Sources

Dog Spirit

p. 3   *the fortieth millennia of our relationship with dogs*: Bob Yirka, "Study Shows Dogs May Have Been Domesticated Far Earlier than Thought," Phys.org, May 15, 2013, https://phys.org/news/2013-05 -dogs-domesticated-earlier-thought.html.

p. 4   *dog attacks account for between thirty and forty deaths*: "Dog Bite Fatalities," DogsBite.org, accessed March 6, 2023, http://www.dogs bite.org/dog-bite-statistics-fatalities.php.

p. 5   *Most attacks are by dogs who are loose*: Janis Bradley, "Dog Bites: Problems and Solutions" (policy paper, Animals and Society Institute, National Canine Research Council, New York, 2014), https://nationalcanineresearchcouncil.com/research_library/dog -bites-problems-solutions-2nd-edition.

p. 5   *snakes kill around ten individuals each year*: "Venomous Snakes," National Institute for Occupational Safety and Health, US Centers for Disease Control and Prevention, accessed March 6, 2023, https://www.cdc.gov/niosh/topics/snakes/default.html.

p. 5   *twenty-seven people killed by mountain lions*: Justin Hoffman, "Here Are All of North America's Recorded Fatal Mountain Lion Attacks," Wide Open Spaces, November 26, 2021, https://www.wideopenspaces.com/fatal-mountain-lion-attacks.

p. 5   *the biggest predators worldwide are mosquitoes*: John Elflein, "Deadliest Animals Globally by Annual Number of Human Deaths 2022," Statista, August 3, 2022, https://www.statista.com/statistics/448169 /deadliest-creatures-in-the-world-by-number-of-human-deaths.

p. 5   *Dolphins, the great apes, a single Asiatic elephant*: Stephanie Gibeault, "Are Dogs Self-Aware? New Research Suggests Yes," American Kennel Club, April 8, 2021, https://www.akc.org/expert-advice /news/a-new-way-to-look-at-dog-self-awareness.

The Legacy of Little Joe

p. 29   *In 1970, one shelter in Eugene, Oregon*: Susan Houser, "The Historical Role of Spay-Neuter in No Kill," Out the Front Door, September 2, 2015, https://www.outthefrontdoor.com/post/the-historical-role -of-spay-neuter-in-no-kill.

Dog Lesson: Wild at Heart

p. 46   *Bees play*: Sofia Quaglia, "Do Bees Play? A Groundbreaking Study Says Yes," *National Geographic*, October 27, 2022, https://www .nationalgeographic.com/animals/article/bees-can-play-study-shows -bumblebees-insect-intelligence.

The Great Horned Owl

p. 60   *our common ancestor, which existed anywhere from 100 million*: Jeff Hecht, "Meet Our Last Common Mammalian Ancestor," *New Scientist*, February 7, 2013, https://www.newscientist.com/article /dn23148-meet-our-last-common-mammalian-ancestor.

p. 60   *Dogs evolved from a now-extinct wolf species*: Krishna Ramanujan, "Study Narrows Origin of Dogs," *Cornell Chronicle* (Cornell University), January 16, 2014, https://news.cornell.edu/stories/2014/01 /study-narrows-origin-dogs.

p. 60   *The Russian scientist Dmitry Belyayev (1917–1985) worked*: Lee Alan Dugatkin, "The Silver Fox Domestication Experiment," *Evolution: Education and Outreach* 11, no. 16 (December 7, 2018), https://evolution-outreach.biomedcentral.com/articles/10.1186 /s12052-018-0090-x.

p. 61   *One researcher, controversially, mused that* Homo sapiens: Pat Shipman, *The Invaders: How Humans and Their Dogs Drove Neanderthals to Extinction* (Cambridge, MA: Belknap Press, 2015).

p. 62   *Dr. Ádám Miklósi, of Eötvös Loránd University*: Ádám Miklósi, "On Dogs and Wolves: The Origin of the Differences," Dog Behavior Blog, October 20, 2008, https://www.dogbehaviorblog.com /2008/10/on-dogs-and-wolves-the-origin-of-the-differences.html.

Dog Lesson: How to Not Get into a Fight

p. 64   *In* Animals Make Us Human, *Temple Grandin notes that wolves*:
Temple Grandin and Catherine Johnson, *Animals Make Us Human:
Creating the Best Life for Animals* (New York: Mariner Books /
Houghton Mifflin Harcourt, 2009).

We Live in a World of Sentience

p. 67   *the psychologist Martin Seligman was researching "learned helplessness"*:
Martin Seligman, *Learned Optimism: How to Change Your Mind and
Your Life* (New York: Vintage Books, 1990/2006).

p. 69   *the fMRI studies of dogs done at Emory University in Atlanta*: Theresa
Fisher, "Brain Scans Reveal What Dogs Really Think of Us," *Mic*,
November 20, 2014 (updated September 13, 2020), https://www
.mic.com/life/brain-scans-reveal-what-dogs-really-think-of-us
-16325834.

p. 70   *To quote the* Encyclopedia of Animal Behavior: D.M. Broom,
"Sentience," in *Encyclopedia of Animal Behavior*, edited by Jae Chun
Choe (Cambridge, MA: Academic Press, 2019), https://www
.sciencedirect.com/topics/neuroscience/sentience.

Dog Lesson: The Importance of Touch

p. 71   *"infants literally cannot survive without human touch"*: Nicole K.
McNichols, "The Vital Importance of Human Touch," *Psychology
Today*, August 3, 2021, https://www.psychologytoday.com/us/blog
/everyone-top/202108/the-vital-importance-human-touch.

A Dog's Reality

p. 74   *Like dogs, bees can't see red, either*: James Bullen, "What Flower
Colours Do Birds and Bees Prefer?," *ABC News Science*, November
15, 2016, https://www.abc.net.au/news/science/2016-11-16/birds
-and-bees-prefer-have-flower-colours-preferences/7959382.

p. 74   *Yet the common house fly sees nearly 250 images*: Stephen Johnson,
"You're Not Fast Enough to Swat a Fly. Here's Why," Big Think,
July 11, 2022, https://bigthink.com/life/the-reason-why-each
-species-experiences-time-differently.

It's Not Just about the Breed

p. 78   *One Chihuahua recently sampled had a genetic link*: Jennifer Raff, *Origin: A Genetic History of the Americas* (New York: Twelve/Hachette, 2022).

p. 85   *Whereas physical traits are good predictors of a dog's breed*: Kathleen Morrill et al., "Ancestry-Inclusive Dog Genomics Challenges Popular Breed Stereotypes," *Science* 376, no. 6592 (April 29, 2022), https://www.science.org/doi/10.1126/science.abk0639.

The Road to Santa Fe

p. 108   *The First People trekked along the shores of ancient*: Kathleen Springer and Jeff Pigati, "The Discovery of Ancient Human Footprints in White Sands National Park and Their Link to Abrupt Climate Change," *Earth Science Matters Newsletter* (USGS; November 30, 2021), https://www.usgs.gov/programs/climate-research-and-development-program/news/discovery-ancient-human-footprints-white.

p. 108   *which is still used in surgeries today*: Peter Shadbolt, "How Stone Age Blades Are Still Cutting It in Modern Surgery," *CNN*, April 2, 2015, https://www.cnn.com/2015/04/02/health/surgery-scalpels-obsidian.

Is It a Good Idea to Have Three Dogs and a Baby in the Wilderness?

p. 121   *Oddly, in 2022, Pope Francis, looking at birth rates declining*: Joshua Berlinger, "Opting for Pets Over Children Is Selfish and 'Takes Away Our Humanity,' Says Pope Francis," *CNN*, January 5, 2022, https://www.cnn.com/2022/01/05/europe/pope-dogs-cats-kids-intl/index.html.

p. 124   *Another study found that, more than half the time*: "Dogs and Kids Are 'in Sync,' Study Shows," Phys.org, February 25, 2021, https://phys.org/news/2021-02-dogs-kids-sync.html.

Zuni Just Wants to Run

p. 131   *The aforementioned Arroyo Hondo was excavated*: Victoria Monagle, Cyler Conrad, and Emily Lena Jones, "What Makes a Dog? Stable

Isotope Analysis and Human-Canid Relationships at Arroyo Hondo Pueblo," *Open Quarternary* 4 (2018), https://openquaternary .com/articles/10.5334/oq.43.

p. 135   *We've been running for two million years*: James Owen, "Humans Were Born to Run, Fossil Study Suggests," *National Geographic*, November 17, 2007, https://www.nationalgeographic.com/science /article/humans-were-born-to-run-fossil-study-suggests.

Dog Lesson: Coyote Fit

p. 136   *Depending on sources, 30 to 50 percent of domestic dogs are obese*: Tony McReynolds, "Pet Obesity Is an Epidemic," *NEWStat* (American Animal Hospital Association), February 6, 2020, https://www.aaha .org/publications/newstat/articles/2020-02/pet-obesity-is-an -epidemic.

Enjoy Chaos? Adopt Bernese Mountain Dog Puppies

p. 158   *One in five individuals bitten by dogs needs medical*: "Dog Bite Prevention," American Veterinary Medical Association, accessed March 6, 2023, https://www.avma.org/resources-tools/pet-owners /dog-bite-prevention.

"Good Nellie, Good Girl"

p. 169   *When they are hurt, even in the name of changing a negative behavior*: Eileen Anderson, "Nine Effects of Punishment," Eileenanddogs .com (blog), September 19, 2014, https://eileenanddogs.com/blog /2014/09/19/effects-punishment.

Dog Lesson: How to Be Old

p. 188   *"I will find myself waist deep in high summer grass"*: Dalia Shevin, "In My Good Death," *The Sun*, October 2010, https://www.thesun magazine.org/issues/418/in-my-good-death; reprinted with permission of the poet.

Rescuing Maisie

p. 201   *women seem unusually interested in men who have small dogs*: Paige Freshwater, "Men with Small Dogs Seen as More Attractive to Women, Study Claims," *Daily Mirror*, August 11, 2022, https://www.mirror.co.uk/news/world-news/men-small-dogs-seen-more-27717615.

Dog Lesson: Resilience

p. 221   *ones I've adapted from a groundbreaking paper by Margaret Haglund*: Margaret Haglund et al., "Six Keys to Resilience for PTSD and Everyday Stress: Teach Patients Protective Attitudes and Behaviors," *Current Psychiatry* 6 (2007), https://www.semanticscholar.org/paper/6-Keys-to-Resilience-for-PTSD-and-Everyday-Stress%3A-Haglund-Cooper/0687e6d17d277461dacad489f0f20ae143e5e155.

Final Lessons

p. 234   *Fourteen thousand years ago, in Germany, an adult couple*: Elyse DeFranco, "How Mythology Could Help Demystify Dog Domestication," *Sciences News*, September 7, 2022, https://www.sciencenews.org/article/dog-domestication-origin-mythology-history.

The Trial of the Pig

p. 235   *In fourteenth-century France, in the village of Falaise*: James McWilliams, "Beastly Justice," *Slate*, February 21, 2013, https://slate.com/human-interest/2013/02/medieval-animal-trials-why-theyre-not-quite-as-crazy-as-they-sound.html.

p. 236   *During this era, issues with wild animals, including moles*: Jen Girgen, "The Historical and Contemporary Prosecution and Punishment of Animals," *Animal Law Review*, Lewis & Clark Law School (2003), https://www.animallaw.info/article/historical-and-contemporary-prosecution-and-punishment-animals.

p. 237   *In the United States today, 99 percent of the animals we consume*:

"Factory Farming," Farm Sanctuary, accessed March 6, 2023,
https://www.farmsanctuary.org/issue/factory-farming.

p. 239   *"It is a mark of modern ignorance to think that we have become"*:
Thomas Goldstein, *Dawn of Modern Science* (Boston: Da Capo
Press, 1980/1995).

p. 239   *which, shockingly, he also conducted with orphaned children*: Theophanes
Avery, "The Most Unethical Science Experiments Conducted on
the Unwitting and Vulnerable," *Owlcation*, April 18, 2023,
https://owlcation.com/humanities/The-Most-Unethical-Science
-Experiments-Conducted-on-the-Unwitting-and-Vulnerable.

p. 240   *Philosopher Mary Anne Warren provided this definition*: Quote by
Mary Anne Warren in Joshua Shepherd, *Consciousness and Moral
Status* (Oxon, UK: Routledge, 2018).

p. 241   *researchers have conducted numerous "inhumane" experiments*: Avery,
"The Most Unethical Science Experiments."

p. 241   *In 2020, over 6.5 million pets were turned over to shelters*: Niall
McCarthy, "Pet Euthanasia Has Declined Sharply in the US,"
Statista, April 11, 2018, https://www.statista.com/chart/13493
/pet-euthanasia-has-declined-sharply-in-the-us.

Dogs of Ukraine

p. 243   *In England, the National Air Raid Precautions Animals Committee*:
"National Air Raid Precautions Animals Committee — NARPAC,"
WW2 Civil Defence Uniforms, Insignia & Equipment, January 28,
2020, https://www.ww2civildefence.co.uk/blog/national-air-raid
-precautions-animals-committee-narpac.

p. 244   *Ukraine is a pet-loving country*: Stanley Coren, "The Value of Pets in
Ukraine During the Russian Invasion," *Psychology Today*, October 4,
2022, https://www.psychologytoday.com/us/blog/canine-corner
/202210/the-value-pets-in-ukraine-during-the-russian-invasion.

p. 245   *In a research paper on the Ukrainian evacuations*: The details from this
research paper are from Coren, "Value of Pets in Ukraine."

Walking in the Universe

p. 248 *From a First People's perspective, according to one encapsulation*: June
Kaminski, "Interconnectedness," First Nations Pedagogy Online,
accessed March 6, 2023, https://firstnationspedagogy.ca
/interconnect.html.

p. 250 *They are the world's decomposers*: University of Bristol, "Scientists Discover When Beetles Became Prolific," Phys.org, March 22, 2022,
https://phys.org/news/2022-03-scientists-beetles-prolific.html.

The World Is a Very Narrow Bridge

p. 259 *If "Heaven is a lovely lake of beer" as St. Bridget wrote*: Barbara
Crooker, "Retriever," in *Selected Poems* (Lexington, KY: FutureCycle
Press, 2015); reprinted with permission from Barbara Crooker.

About the Author

Hersch Wilson is a writer and dog guardian who lives in Santa Fe, New Mexico. His family adopted their first dog, Shawnee, a German shepherd, when Hersch was ten. Since then, apart from a few dogless periods, he has been around dogs for over sixty years.

Hersch has worked as a dancer, a pilot, a soccer coach, and a leadership consultant. In 2022 he retired after thirty-three years as a volunteer assistant chief with the Santa Fe County Fire Department. His book *Firefighter Zen: A Field Guide to Thriving in Tough Times* was published in 2020 and won numerous awards.

He has written several other books, including *Play to Win: Choosing Growth over Fear* (with his father, Larry Wilson) and a self-published novel *Test of Faith: A Novel of Faith and Murder in the Southwest*.

His partner of forty-four years, Laurie, owns the renowned pet boutique Teca Tu in the heart of Santa Fe — she sees a lot of dogs! They have two animal-loving adult daughters, Brynne and Sully, and two grandchildren, Fiona and Dash. Of course, the Wilson household is a "forever home" to two dogs: Toby, a Great Pyrenees; and Maisie, a Chihuahua-terrier mix.

More of Hersch's work can be found at his website HerschWilson.com and on Medium.com (HerschWilson.Medium.com).